Making Great
Handmade Cards

IT'S EASIER THAN YOU THINK

YOU DID IT!

WAY TO GO!

HAPPY BIRTHDAY

Includes:
- instructions for 124 cards
- 32 card-making techniques
- 32 acid-free & lignin-free patterned sheets
- papers for 21 cards

HOT OFF THE PRESS INC

HOTP 2272

Shauna Berglund-Immel   *Susan Cobb*   *Leane de Graaf*   *Lisa Garcia-Bergstedt*   *LeNae Gerig*

Card Designers:

Shauna Berglund-Immel works for Hot Off The Press as a Scrapbook Specialist and in-house designer. Shauna and her husband, Dave, live in Oregon with their children, Spencer and Kaelin.

Susan Cobb is a talented Hot Off The Press designer, Scrapbook Specialist and technical editor. She lives in Oregon with her husband, Brian, their two daughters and their two cats.

Leane de Graaf lives in the Netherlands with her husband and two cats. She specializes in tea bag folding and beading techniques.

Lisa Garcia-Bergstedt is the newest Scrapbook Specialist for Hot Off The Press. She lives in Oregon with her husband, Kurt, their son, Griffin, and their cat, Mao.

LeNae Gerig is an in-house designer, Scrapbook Specialist and technical editor. She lives in Oregon with her husband, Chris, their daughter, Lauren, and their dog, Bailey.

Amy Gustafson offers her talents to Hot Off The Press whether she's residing in Oregon or France. She is a Scrapbook Specialist, calligrapher and paper crafter.

Teresa Nelson is Vice-President of Hot Off The Press. She's written over 50 books on subjects as diverse as floral design, weddings, appliqué, fabric painting, jewelry, giftwrapping and scrapbooking. She lives in Oregon.

Amy Gustafson

Teresa Nelson

Production Credits:

President: Paulette Jarvey
Vice-President: Teresa Nelson
Production Manager: Lynda Hill
Project Editors: Sherry Harbert, Victoria Weber
Technical Editors: Shauna Berglund-Immel, Rosemary Hands, Liz Hing
Photographer: John McNally
Graphic Designers: Jacie Pete, Joy Schaber
Editors: Paulette Jarvey, Teresa Nelson, Lynda Hill
Digital Imagers: Victoria Weber, Gretchen Putman

published by:

HOT OFF THE PRESS INC.

Hot Off The Press wants to be kind to the environment. Whenever possible we follow the 3 R's—reduce, reuse and recycle. We use soy and UV inks that greatly reduce the release of volatile organic solvents.

For a color catalog of nearly 800 products, send $2.00 to:

HOT OFF THE PRESS INC.
1250 N.W. Third, Dept. B
Canby, Oregon 97013
phone (503) 266-9102
fax (503) 266-8749
http://www.craftpizazz.com

Making Great
Handmade Cards

IT'S EASIER THAN YOU THINK

Table of Contents

Table of Contents

You'll love card-making. As you can see, we do too. There's just something creative and wonderful about taking a few pieces of paper and turning them into a beautiful, whimsical or charming paper message. And by making your own cards, they'll perfectly state the message you want to give. This book is the second in a series. The first, *How To Create Handmade Cards If You Think You Can't*, was a bestseller. The thank you letters (and cards) encouraged us to further develop the paper engineering we created in that book. *Making Great Handmade Cards* is the result.

In these pages, you'll find new versions of old favorites, such as tea bag folding and collage—and we've developed many new techniques for card-making. Pin-pricking and beading are two techniques that produce gorgeous cards—a little extra time is required, but the results are well worth the effort!

There are more 3-dimensional focals to create—from score-and-fold embellishments to pop-ups. Skeleton leaves, wire and special cuts dress up ordinary cards and make them special keepsakes. And to make sure everyone can enjoy this book, we've included all the basic card-making instructions, too.

Go ahead, pick some projects and get started. In the back of the book, there are papers to make 21 cards (they are indicated in the material's list with the words "patterned papers in this book".) But, be careful—paper engineering and card-making may be habit forming!

Beading

Beading is an exciting new addition to card making, especially with Leane's beautiful designs! Although it may look complicated, just follow the diagrams 1, 2, 3... Be sure to use a needle that will fit inside the beads and stay within the diagram points for a perfect look every time.

by Leane de Graaf

- 5"x6½" Paper Flair™ white blank card
- Paper Flair™ Blossoms & Buds Paper Pack
- solid lavender paper
- 48 metallic dark jewel-colored ¼" bugle beads
- 96 blue ¹⁄₁₆" glass seed beads
- purple thread, sewing needle
- cardiff corner punch (Family Treasures)
- tracing paper, transfer paper

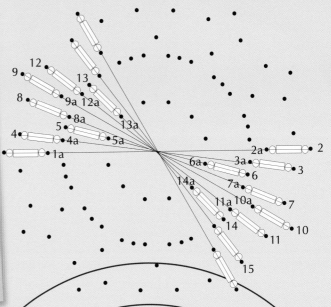

circle patterns

1 Cover the card front with lavender paper. Cut a 4⅞"x6¼" rectangle of purple hydrangeas; glue it centered on the card front. Cut a 4⅝" square of lavender. Use the punch at each corner. Glue it centered on the card front.

2 Cut a 3⅝" circle of lavender and mat it onto a 4½" circle of purple hydrangeas. Trace and transfer the beading pattern dots above, centered on the back of the matted circle. Use a pencil and ruler to draw the straight lines as guides for beading; write the numbers to mark the points, if desired.

3 Thread the needle with purple thread, knotting the end. Insert it into point #1 on the circle back and pull it to the front. Slip a bead combination of one seed, one bugle and another seed bead onto the thread, pushing them against the paper, then insert the needle into point #1a, pulling it to the back. Reinsert the needle into point #1, then through the beads.

4 Before inserting the needle through point #2, slip on the identical bead combination, pushing them against #2 insertion point. Insert the needle into point #2a, through the beads and back into point #2, pulling it to the back. Repeat the beading process at point #3 and continue to form the circle pattern. Glue the beaded circle centered on the card front.

- *5"x6½" Paper Flair™ ivory blank card*
- *Paper Flair™ White, Cream & Laser Lace Petite Prints™ Paper Pack*
- *2½"x3⅝" rectangle of ivory cardstock*
- *16 gold ¼" bugle beads*
- *56 metallic copper ¹⁄₁₆" glass seed beads*
- *metallic copper thread, sewing needle*
- *tracing paper, transfer paper*

1 Cover the card front with the swirls paper. Cut a 2¾"x6½" rectangle of tan fleckled paper and glue it centered on the card front. Cut two 2½"x1" rectangles of swirls and glue to the flecked paper, one ¼" from the top edge and the other ¼" from the bottom edge.

2 Transfer the beading pattern on page 79 centering it on the ivory cardstock back. Thread the needle with copper thread, knotting the end. Insert the needle into point #1 on the rectangle back and pull it to the front, then insert the needle into point B, pulling it to the back. Insert the needle up through point #2 on the back and pull it to the front, then down through point B. Repeat this process through point #10. Reinsert the needle through point #10, then into point A. Repeat the process through point #19. Turn the rectangle and duplicate the process for points #1a through #19a.

by Leane de Graaf

3 Insert the needle into point #1 on the rectangle back and pull it to the front. Thread the beads as shown on the bead pattern; then insert the needle into point #10. Repeat for beading between points #2 and #9, #3 and #8, #4 and #7 and #5 and #6; then duplicate the process for points #10 through #19. Insert the needle into point #1a, then reinsert it into point #10a. Repeat the process between points #2a and #9a, #3a and #8a and #4a and #7a. Insert the needle into #5a, slip three rocaille beads onto the thread, then insert the needle into #6a. Duplicate the process for points #19a through #10a. Glue the beaded rectangle to the card front as shown.

by Leane de Graaf

- *5"x6½" Paper Flair™ white blank card*
- *Paper Flair™ Blossoms & Buds Paper Pack*
- *2"x3³⁄₁₆" rectangle of ivory cardstock*
- *solid white paper*
- *4 green ¼" bugle beads*
- *96 green ¹⁄₁₆" glass seed beads*
- *dark green thread, sewing needle*
- *tracing paper, transfer paper*

1 Cut a 4¾"x6¼" rectangle of ferns and glue it centered on the card front. Cut a 3⅞"x5¼" rectangle of white roses and mat on white, leaving a ¹⁄₁₆" border; glue it centered to the card front.

2 Transfer the beading pattern on page 79, centering it on the ivory cardstock back. Thread the needle with green thread, knotting the end. Insert the needle into point A on the rectangle back and pull it to the front, then insert the needle into point B, pulling it to the back. Insert the needle back into point A, slip one seed bead onto the thread, then insert the needle into point #1. Secure the bead in place by inserting the needle into point #1a, then through the bead and back into point #1. Continue the process using the bead pattern in the diagram with A as the anchor through point #11. Repeat the process for the lower right corner, using B as the anchor.

3 Repeat the stitching and beading process for the upper corners, using A as the anchor for the left side and B for the right side. Glue the beaded rectangle centered on the card front.

Chalking

Chalking is a simple yet beautiful way to enhance images on cards. They're especially effective on laser cuts and embossed paper motifs. For best results, use a chalk with concentrated pigment (not blackboard chalk)—we like Craf-T chalks. Use a cotton swab or make-up sponge applicator and lightly apply the chalk to your image. Use your finger to blend the colors to get just the right results, then seal the chalk with a fixative—we recommend Blair No-Odor Spray. Once you've tried it, you'll look for ways to add chalking to your cards. Have fun!

by Amy Gustafson

- *5"x6½" Paper Flair™ white blank card*
- *patterned papers in this book*
- *pink, blue, yellow, green decorating chalks (Craf-T Products)*
- *chalk fixative (Blair)*
- *black pen (Sakura® Gelly Roll™)*

1⅛" square

1 Cut the card to 5" square. Cut four 1⅛" squares each from the following papers: pink dots, blue mesh, yellow stripes, green swirls. Arrange them on the card front in four rows of four columns as shown, leaving ¹⁄₁₆" between the squares and around the outside edges. Cut out the hearts. Glue them centered on the squares along the edge of the card front as shown above.

2 With the black pen, draw 8-9 stitch marks on each side of each square and 10-11 stitch marks around each heart; then outline each square and heart in black. Use the matching color chalk per square color to darken the edges around each heart square.

3 Cut out the verse "Friends are like quilts...they are a great source of comfort!" Glue it centered on the card front.

- 5"x6½" Paper Flair™ white blank card
- Paper Flair™ Teal Petite Prints™ Paper Pack
- solid papers: yellow, white
- Paper Flair™ Laser Motifs Card Embellishments
- yellow, green, brown and black decorating chalks: Craf-T Products
- chalk fixative (Blair)
- X-acto® knife, cutting surface

1 Cut the card to 5" square. Cover the card front with the dark teal dotted paper. Cut a 3¾" square of the dark teal stripe paper and mat it on yellow, leaving a ¹⁄₁₆" border. Glue it centered on the card front.

2 Cut out the sunflower motif and apply chalks to the image as shown. Mat the sunflower on white paper, leaving a ¹⁄₁₆" border. Mat it again on yellow, leaving a ¹⁄₁₆" border. Glue the matted motif on the card front.

by Amy Gustafson

by Lisa Garcia-Bergstedt

- 5"x6½" Paper Flair™ white blank card
- Paper Flair™ Soft Patterns Paper Pack
- Paper Flair™ Laser Words Card Embellishments
- solid white paper
- lavender, purple decorating chalks (Craf-T Products)
- chalk fixative (Blair)
- 24" of ¼" wide lavender satin ribbon (Offray®)
- X-acto® knife, cutting surface
- mini glue dots (Glue Dots, Inc.)

1 Cut a 6"x4½" rectangle from the green flowered paper. Glue it centered on the card front. Cut a 5"x3½" rectangle from the lavender leaves paper; mat it on white, leaving a ¹⁄₁₆" border. Glue it centered on the flowered paper.

2 Draw a 3¾"x2" rectangle onto the center of the card front. Open the card face up on a cutting surface. Use the X-acto® knife to cut out the window.

3 Cut out the laser embellishment to a 4"x2⅛" rectangle. Use the purple chalk to highlight the letters and the lavender chalk to lightly highlight the leaves and border. Glue the embellishment to the inside front, so it shows through the window.

4 Cut an 8" length of ribbon, cutting the ends at an angle. Center it over the window top, then fold each end over to frame the left and right sides. Cut the remaining ribbon in half. Use each half to make a shoestring bow and glue one to each upper corner as shown.

Christmas

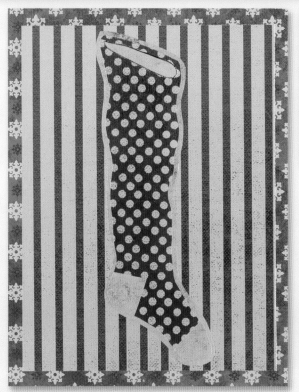

by Lisa Garcia-Bergstedt

- 5"x6½" Paper Flair™ white blank card
- Paper Flair™ Blue & Silver Christmas Paper Pack
- X-acto® knife
- cutting surface
- tracing paper
- transfer paper

1 Cover the card front with the small silver and blue snowflake paper. Cut a 4½"x5⅞" rectangle of the silver and blue stripe paper. Glue it centered on the card front.

2 Using the pattern cut out a stocking from silver dots on blue paper. Mat on solid silver paper and trim, leaving a ¹⁄₁₆" edge. Cut the accent pieces from the solid silver paper and glue on the stocking. Glue it to the card front.

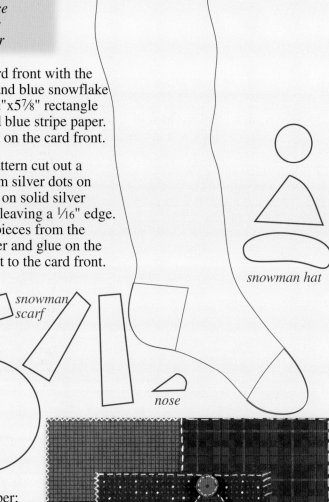

snowman hat

snowman scarf

nose

- 5"x6½" Paper Flair™ white blank card
- Paper Flair™ Christmas Flannels Paper Pack
- solid papers: white, orange
- Paper Flair™ Christmas Laser Greetings Card Embellishments
- white pen (Pentel Milky Gel Roller)
- foam adhesive tape
- X-acto® knife, cutting surface
- tracing paper, transfer paper

1 Cut out the following: one 2½" square from red/green plaid paper; one 2½"x1½" rectangle from green mesh, one 1½"x2¾" rectangle from red/green plaid, one 2½" square from blue/green/red plaid, one 2½" square and one 1½" square from red/blue dots on green paper. Arrange the pieces overlapping along the outer edge of card front, and glue in place. Cut a 3"x4" rectangle from red/green dots on blue paper, and glue to the center of the card front.

2 Use the patterns to cut out a hat, scarf, hat ball, trim and the carrot nose from papers as shown. Tear out the snowman pieces and snow mound from white. Use foam tape to adhere the snowman and hat to the card as shown. Cut ¼" slits along the scarf ends to form fringe; glue the scarf and nose to the snowman as shown. Use the black pen to draw the eyes, mouth and buttons.

3 Cut out the "Let it Snow" laser motif, then carefully tear the top edge near the snowflakes. Glue it below the snow mound on the card front as shown. Use the white pen to add stitching and zig-zag details to the patchwork pieces and to the snowman's hat and scarf; add white "snow" dots around the snowman.

snow mound

by Susan Cobb

- *5"x6½" Paper Flair™ ivory blank card*
- *Paper Flair™ Burgundy & Gold Christmas Paper Pack*
- *Paper Flair™ Windows #1 Template*
- *gold pen (Pentel Hybrid Gel Roller)*
- *8" length of metallic gold thread, sewing needle*
- *⅜" wide hole punch (Marvy® Uchida)*
- *foam adhesive tape*
- *X-acto® knife, cutting surface*
- *tracing paper, transfer paper*

tag

card inside

by Susan Cobb

1 Cover the card front with gold sponged paper. Cut a 4½"x6" rectangle from the gold holly leaves on burgundy paper and glue it centered on the card front. Use the template to draw the four 1" squares positioned as shown to form windows. Open the card face up on a cutting surface and use the X-acto® knife to cut out the windows. Open the card and cover the inside back with the burgundy dots on gold paper.

2 Cut four ¼"x5" strips from gold sponged paper, and glue each pair back to back. Cut one in half. Cut a "V" at one end of each of the other two pieces; glue the straight ends together at an angle at the top of the window. Cut the remaining strip in half, then pull all the ends together and attach over the first strips as shown for a bow. Punch a circle from sponged gold paper and adhere it to the center of the bow with foam tape.

3 Use the pattern to cut an ivory tag, then mat on sponged gold, leaving a ¹⁄₁₆" border. Pierce a hole in one end with the needle, then thread both ends of the gold thread through the hole. Pull the ends through the resulting loop, and pull tight. Trim the threads to 1", and glue the ends under the gold bow as show. Cut a 3"x2" piece of ivory paper and mat on burgundy holly paper, trimming edges to a ½" border. Glue to the lower half of the inside back. Write "Joy" on the tag, and "May you unwrap the joy of the season every day of the year" on the rectangle with the gold pen.

small card inside

by Susan Cobb

- *5"x6½" Paper Flair™ white blank card*
- *Paper Flair™ Christmas Brights Paper Pack*
- *solid papers: yellow, red*
- *Paper Flair™ Christmas Embossed Designs Card Embellishments*
- *gold pen (Pentel Hybrid Gel Roller)*
- *X-acto® knife, cutting surface*

1 Cover the card front with red sponged paper. Cut a 4¾"x6¼" rectangle from snowflake/dots on green paper and glue to the center of the card front. Cut a 3⅝"x5⅛" rectangle from red sponged paper, and mat on green checked paper, leaving a ¼" border with two rows of checks on each side. Mat it again on yellow, leaving a ¹⁄₁₆" border. Glue it centered on the card front.

2 Cut three 1" squares from the green checked paper; then cut each square in half diagonally. Glue the triangles to the top and bottom edges of the red sponged rectangle, spaced as shown. Cut a 5½"x2¾" piece from the snowflakes/dots paper and fold in half to make a small card. Mat on yellow paper, trimming to a ¹⁄₁₆" border. Glue to the center of the card front.

3 Cut out the embossed drum in a 2" square; mat on red, leaving a ¹⁄₁₆" border. Glue to the front of the small card. Use the gold pen to write "Jolly Holidays" on the card front as shown and your own special message inside the mini card.

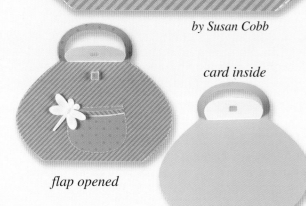

by Susan Cobb

card inside

flap opened

1. Cut out the patterned purse pieces. Glue the pink stripes purse on the card front, so the bottom edge is aligned with the card fold. Place the card on a cutting surface and use the X-acto® knife to cut out the outer purse shape. Glue the turquoise purse shape to the inside back. Close the card, then use the X-acto® knife to cut just the solid white line. Open the card face up and cut along the bottom edge inside the handle on the card front only. Use the dull edge of the knife to score along the bottom edge of the handle on the inside back and fold through the handle to the front.

- *5"x6½" Paper Flair™ white blank card*
- *patterned papers in this book*
- *white pen (Pentel Milky Gel Roller)*
- *X-acto® knife, cutting surface*
- *foam adhesive tape*
- *tracing paper, transfer paper*

2. Cover the card front handle and the card back flap in the pink dots on turquoise paper. Glue the pink stripes buckle centered on the front flap. Open the card face up on a cutting surface, with the flap open; cut out the inner ¼" square of the buckle. Close the card, folding over the flap and lightly draw the inner square on the purse base; attach two layers of ¼" squares of foam tape on the drawn square. Cover the foam tape with the pink dot on turquoise square.

3. Glue the purse pocket centered on the purse front as shown. Glue the pink stripes stripe on the pocket. Glue the dragonfly motif to the top left corner of the pocket. With the white pen, apply stitch marks to the purse front flap and pocket; outline the handle, buckle and stripes strip on the pocket.

- *5"x6½" Paper Flair™ white blank card*
- *Paper Flair™ Blue Petite Prints™ Paper Pack*
- *white pen (Marvy® Uchida)*
- *⅛" wide hole punch (McGill)*
- *3 clear blue ¼" pony beads*
- *36" length of twine*
- *X-acto® knife, cutting surface*

1. Open the card face down on a cutting surface and vertically score 2½" in from each side. Cut off 1" from each side, then fold on the scored lines. Cover both panel fronts in blue clover paper. Cut a 5"x6½" rectangle from blue dots paper. Cut a 5½" square from the dark blue flowers paper; fold under ½" along one edge. Glue this folded section face down to the inside back, centered along the left panel fold line. Glue the dotted piece to cover to the inside back, then fold the flowered flap over it.

2. With the white pen, outline the flowered square and write "Thinking of You" on the inside back, centered 2" below the top edge of the card. Open the front panels and punch three holes on each, ⅛" from the side edge, and exactly 1¼" above the bottom edge, 3¼" from the bottom and 1¼" below the top edge. Cut the twine into 6" lengths. Fold one length in half and tie a knot ½" from the ends. Insert this loop through a hole on the right panel. Repeat for the other two holes.

3. Cut one piece of twine in half and knot two ends together. Thread the two strands through a bead, then thread it through a hole on the left panel; tie a knot on the front. Repeat with the other two beads. Close the card and pull each bead through the loop directly to its right.

panels opened

card inside

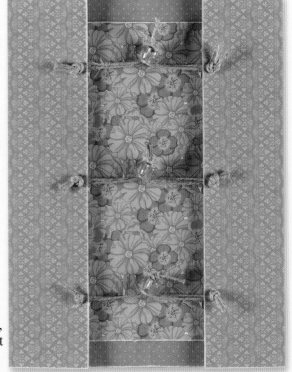

by Amy Gustafson

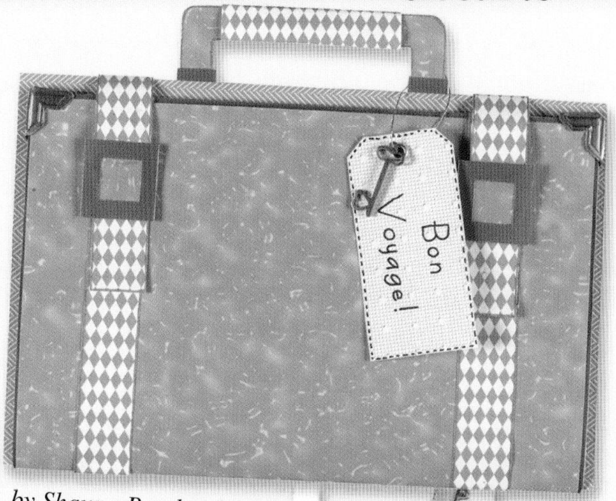

by Shauna Berglund-Immel

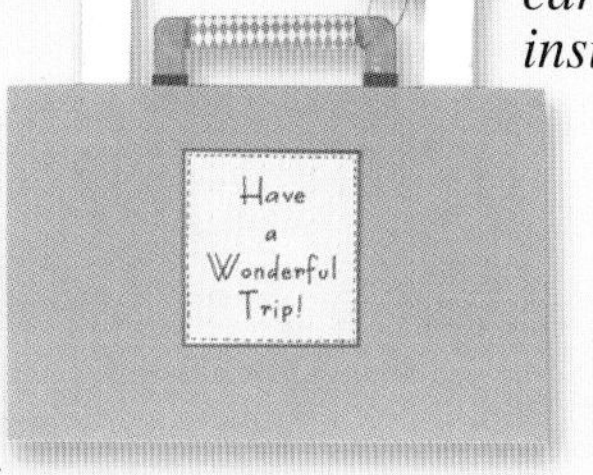

card inside

- *5"x6½" Paper Flair™ white blank card*
- *Paper Flair™ White, Cream & Laser Lace Petite Prints™ Paper Pack*
- *Paper Flair™ Gold Patterns Paper Pack*
- *gold pen (Pentel Hybrid Gel Roller)*
- *black pen (Sakura® Gelly Roll™)*
- *gold key charm*
- *metallic gold thread*
- *gold photo corners (Canson)*
- *gold eyelet (Stamp Studio)*
- *X-acto® knife, cutting surface*
- *tracing paper, transfer paper*

1 Transfer the suitcase pattern on page 77 onto the card and cut out. Cover the handle with tan flecked paper, then wrap a 2"x¾" rectangle of diamonds around the handle top. Cover the card front with tan herringbone paper. Cut a 4¼"x6¼" rectangle of tan flecked; mat it on gold, leaving a 1/16" border. Fold ½" along the long edge and glue the fold to the back of the card so the flecked paper wraps to the front. Glue a photo corner to each top corner of the flecked flap.

2 Cut two ⅝"x11" strips from the diamonds paper; outline the edges in gold pen. Fold under ⅛" at one end of a strip and glue it on the inside front of the flecked flap ¾" from the left edge. Wrap the strip around the front and onto the back of the card, with 2⅜" extending up from the left side of the handle; glue. Repeat with the other strip on the right side of the handle.

3 With the black pen, write "Have a Wonderful Trip" on a 2"x2¼" rectangle of lace netting paper and mat it on gold, leaving a 1/16" border. Draw dashes along the edges with the black pen and glue it to the herringbone, centered between the handles. Transfer the tag onto the lace netting and cut it out. Draw dashes along the edges and write "Bon Voyage!" Attach an eyelet at the tag top; thread the charm and tag onto the thread and tie it around the right handle and knot.

4 Cut two ½"x⅛" strips of gold and glue one to each handle base. Outline the handle in gold pen. Cut two 1½"x½" strips of tan flecked; fold the ends together to form a ¾" wide flat tube. Glue it (with the tube opened at the top and bottom) ¾" from the top edge of the left diamonds strip on the card front. Repeat for the right side. Cut two ⅞" square gold buckles and glue one on top of each tube. Cut a ½" square of flecked and glue it centered on the buckle; repeat for the other buckle. Wrap the diamond straps over the front and slip through the tubes.

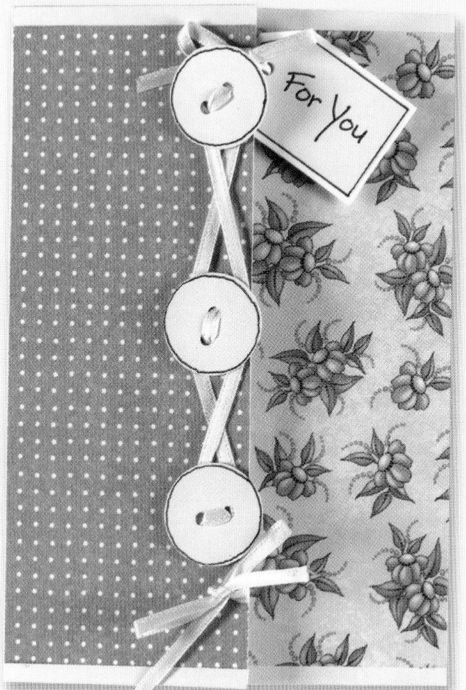

by Susan Cobb

- *5"x6½" Paper Flair™ white blank card*
- *white cardstock*
- *Paper Flair™ Soft Patterns Paper Pack*
- *pale yellow paper*
- *1½ yards of ⅛" wide ivory satin ribbon (Offray®)*
- *⅛" wide hole punch (McGill)*
- *1" wide hole punch (Family Treasures, Inc.)*
- *foam adhesive tape*
- *black pen (Zig® Writer)*
- *X-acto® knife*
- *cutting surface*

1 Open the card face down on a cutting surface and score 2½" on the left side and 3" on the right; fold in the panels. Cover the left panel with green with white dots paper and the right panel with purple flowers on yellow paper. Cut the tag from yellow, mat it on cardstock, leaving a 1/16" border.

2 Cut ⅛" wide strips from the yellow paper and glue along the tops and bottoms of the panels. Glue a 1½"x4" rectangle of yellow to the cardstock; then punch three 1" circles. Punch two ⅛" circles ¼" apart in each circle center, one in the tag, then at ¾", 1", 3", 5" and 5½" from the top on the left panel. Punch two holes ¼" apart ¾" from the top and bottom of the right panel. Use the black pen to outline the buttons and tag and write "For You".

3 Cut the ribbon in the following lengths: three 6", two 10" and one 16". Thread a 6" length through a button, then through the 1" hole on the left panel and knot in back. Repeat with the other buttons. Weave the 16" around the buttons and knot. Thread one 10" ribbon from the inside of the right panel, through the tag and top left panel hole and tie in a shoestring bow. Repeat with the remaining ribbon for the bottom hole.

Collage

Collage is a fun way to mix your favorite patterns, shapes and embellishments in paper crafting. We've designed cards to highlight some of the most popular techniques used in cardmaking just for you. Lisa mixed a variety of patterned papers, then added some fun embellishments to make her ideas come alive. On page 17, Amy spiced up her garden card by cutting out her favorite flowers and overlapping them for a spectacular effect. Susan used paper quilting (see more quilting ideas on pages 48 and 49) to show how the collage technique works well when mixing colors and shapes. So, step away from the traditional use of single-color combinations and show your colorful side. Have fun!

by Lisa Garcia-Bergstedt

- 5"x6½" Paper Flair™ ivory blank card
- Paper Flair™ White, Cream & Laser Lace Petite Prints™ Paper Pack
- Paper Flair™ Pink Petite Prints™ Paper Pack
- solid pale yellow paper
- black pen: Sakura® 3mm Micron
- 20" of ¹⁄₁₆" wide yellow satin ribbon (Offray®)
- tortoise-shell buttons: one ¹³⁄₁₆", one ⅝", two ½", one ⁷⁄₁₆", one ⁵⁄₁₆"
- foam adhesive tape

1 Trim 1¼" off the open edge of the card front. Cut a 6½"x¼" strip of the pink stripes paper and glue it along the open edge of the card front. Cut a 6½"x3⅝" rectangle of ivory dots and glue to the card front, allowing ¹⁄₁₆" of the stripes to show.

2 Cut a 6½"x4" rectangle of pale yellow. Glue it to the inside front, even with the fold; then tear the edge so it extends ¼" beyond the card front edge. Cover the inside back with ivory/tan diamonds paper.

3 Cut three 1⅞" squares of pink stripes; mat each on pale yellow, leaving a ¹⁄₁₆" border. Tear three 3"x¾" strips of tan flecks paper. Wrap one strip around the center of each square, gluing the ends at the back. Glue them to the card front evenly spaced as shown.

4 Thread ribbon through the holes on the large button and knot it on top; trim the ribbon ends to ⅜". Repeat for each remaining button, trimming the ribbon ends to ¼"; set the three smaller buttons aside. Use foam tape to attach the largest button to the center square. Repeat with a button on the other two squares.

5 Cut three 1" squares of pale yellow. Tear three 1½"x⅝" strips of tan flecks and wrap one around each yellow square, gluing the ends at the back. Cut three 1¼"x¹⁄₁₆" strips of pink stripes and wrap one around the center of each tan fleck strip, gluing the ends at the back.

6 Use foam tape to attach a button to each square, then glue the squares evenly spaced on the inside back as shown. With the black pen, write "thinking of you" on the card front below the pink squares.

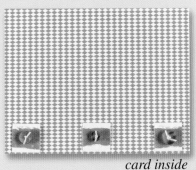

card inside

16

- *5"x6½" Paper Flair™ white blank card*
- *Paper Flair™ Blossoms & Buds Paper Pack*
- *Paper Flair™ Pastel Vellum Paper Pack*
- *gold pen (Sakura® Gelly Roll™)*

1 Cut a 5"x6½" rectangle from the white daisies paper. Place it on a cutting surface and use the X-acto® knife to cut around some of the petals on 4-5 daisies. Glue the sides and bottom of the white daisies paper to the card front.

2 Cut out varying sizes of flowers from the yellow daisies paper and leaves from the green ivy paper. Glue them randomly on the card front, slipping some behind the slits on the white daisies paper.

3 Cut a 3¼"x6" rectangle of blue vellum paper; fold ½" under on the top (short) edge. Place the fold between the top of the card front and the white daisies paper; glue along the top edge to secure. With the gold pen, write "A friend is the greatest of all blessings!" centered on the vellum flap. Carefully glue the flap in place near the lower edge.

A
true
friend
is
the
greatest
of
all
blessings!

by Amy Gustafson

by Susan Cobb

- *5"x6½" Paper Flair™ ivory blank card*
- *patterned papers in this book*
- *9" of ¼" wide pale peach satin ribbon (Offray®)*
- *mini glue dots (Glue Dots Inc.)*

1 Cover the card front with the peach florets paper. Cut out the following shapes from the peach plaid paper: 1¾" square, 1⅛"x5" strip, ¾"x6½" strip. Cut out a 4" square and a 1" square from the floral peach stripes paper; mat each on pale yellow, leaving a 1/16" border. Cut out a 2"x3¼" rectangle from the floral yellow stripes paper; mat on pale yellow, leaving a 1/16" border.

2 With the card fold at the top, glue the wide plaid strip 1⅛" from the left side. Glue the matted floral peach stripes with the left edge placed in the center of the plaid strip. Cut a ¼"x6½" strip of pale yellow and glue it across the center of the narrow plaid strip, then glue the strip horizontally across the center of the card front. Glue the floral yellow stripes rectangle 1½" from the right edge as shown.

3 Glue the matted 1" square centered on the plaid square. Turn it on point to make a diamond and glue it on top of the yellow stripes rectangle as shown. Tie the ribbon into a shoestring bow with 1" loops and attach it with a glue dot near the left edge of the card as shown.

Dangle

There's a fun surprise in each of these cards—something dangles in a window on the front. It's a wonderful technique!

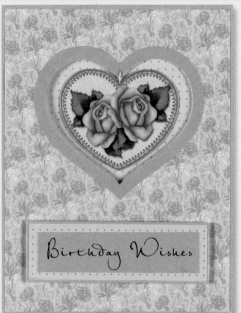

1 Cover the card front with pink. Cut a 4¾"x6⅜" rectangle of roses paper and glue it centered on the pink front. Cut out the heart window and glue it on the front 1" below the top card edge. Open the card face up on a cutting surface; use an X-acto® knife to cut out the center of the window (along the blue line).

2 Cut out the "Birthday Wishes" message and mat it on the dots, leaving a ⅛" border. Mat it again on pink, leaving a 1/16" border. Use foam tape to attach it to the card front ¾" from the lower edge.

3 Open the card and cover the inside back with blue dots. Cut out the "Just for You!" message heart and glue it to the dots, centered in the window when the card is closed. Cut out both rose hearts. Use a needle to thread the silver thread through the card front at the top of the heart. Bring the ends together and glue them between the two hearts, trim any exposed thread ends if needed.

- 5"x6½" Paper Flair™ white blank card
- patterned papers in this book
- 6" silver metallic thread
- sewing needle
- X-acto® knife, cutting surface
- foam adhesive tape

card inside

by Teresa Nelson

- 5"x6½" Paper Flair™ white blank card
- Paper Flair™ Purple Petite Prints™ Paper Pack
- solid papers: lavender, white
- Paper Flair™ Windows #1, Windows #2 Templates
- white pen (Pentel Milky Gel Roller)
- black pen (Zig® Millenium)
- 9" of silver thread, sewing needle
- 2" of 24-gauge silver wire, pliers
- X-acto® knife, cutting surface

1 Cut the card to 5" square. Cover the card front and inside back with the purple dots. Cut a 4½" square from lavender stars paper; mat it on lavender, leaving a 1/16" border. Glue it centered on the card front.

2 Open card face up on a cutting surface. Use the template to draw a 2" square 1¼" from the top edge of the card front. Use the X-acto® knife to cut out the window. Glue the cut square to the inside back, so it is centered in the window of the card front. Use the white pen to outline the edge of the window.

by Susan Cobb

3 Use the template to draw two 1½" stars on lavender stars paper; glue the backs together. Repeat to make a double-sided star from purple dots. Make a ¾" slit from the top point of the lavender stars star toward its center and a ⅝" slit from the bottom center of the dots star toward its center. Slide the stars together along the slits.

4 Wrap the wire around the needle in a spiral. Remove the wire. Use the sewing needle to pierce a hole through the star top, then thread the wire through it and crimp it to secure. Use the needle to pierce another hole above the window; insert the other end of the wire and crimp it closed on the inside front.

5 Tie the thread in a shoestring bow. Glue it on the card front as shown. Use the black pen to write "Congratulations, Graduate!" on a 2"x⅞" lavender rectangle; mat it on purple dots, leaving a 1/16" border. Glue it to the card front below the window. Write "Keep reaching for the stars!" on a 3¼"x¾" rectangle of lavender; mat it on purple dots and on lavender, each with a 1/16" border. Glue it to the inside back below the lavender stars square.

card inside

- *5"x6½" Paper Flair™ white blank card*
- *patterned papers in this book*
- *8" of 30-gauge gold wire*
- *sewing needle*
- *X-acto® knife, cutting surface*

card inside

And feel better soon!

1 Cover the card front with aqua paper. Cut a
4¾"x6⅛" rectangle of yellow checks paper and
glue it centered on the card front. Cut out the aqua rectangular
window and glue it to the card front ¾" from the top edge. Open
the card and place it face up on a cutting surface. Use the X-acto®
knife to cut out the window along the white line.

2 Cut out both bug images and glue them back-to-back, without
gluing the hands. Use the needle to pierce a hole through the
upper corners of the window. Thread wire through the holes and
twist the ends together at the center front. Wrap each side of the
hands over the wire to conceal the center twist, then glue the hands
together.

3 Cut out the "Hang in there!" message and mat it on aqua,
leaving a ¹/₁₆" border. Glue it to the card front as shown. Open
the card and cover the inside back with yellow swirls. Cut out the
"And feel better soon!" message; mat it on aqua, leaving a ¹/₁₆"
border. Glue it on the inside back, below the window so it's hidden
when the card is closed.

Hang in there!

art by Annie Lang; card by Teresa Nelson

by Shauna Berglund-Immel

1 Cut a 5"x2¾" rect-
angle of gold dots.
Punch a hole in the two
top corners. Cut a 7"
length of thread. Insert
one end of the thread
through the right hole;
use tape to secure the
end at the back. Thread
the four beads onto the
thread, then insert the
other end into the left hole and tape at the back.

- *5"x6½" Paper Flair™ white blank card*
- *Paper Flair™ Gold Patterns Paper Pack*
- *black pen (Sakura® Gelly Roll™)*
- *10" of gold thread*
- *four 4mm iridescent faceted beads (Blue Moon Beads)*
- *¹/₁₆" hole punch (McGill. Inc.)*
- *foam adhesive tape*
- *tracing paper, transfer paper*
- *clear adhesive tape*

2 Use the triangle pattern below to cut three triangles from the gold
dots on purple. Fold under ⅛" along the bottom of each triangle and
trim the excess at the corners. Wrap the fold over the thread between two
beads, with the patterned side in front. Use tape on the back side to secure
the triangle to the thread. Repeat for the remaining triangles.

3 Glue the gold dots rectangle to the top portion of the card front.
Cover the bottom portion with gold flourishes on purple. Cut a 5"x¼"
strip of gold and glue it centered between the two papers.

4 Cut one 1½"x2¼" and one 3"x1½" rectangle from the gold roses
paper. Cut ¼" wide strips of gold and glue them to the rectangles as
shown. Cut a ¼"x3½" strip of gold; fold it into three loops and glue it to the top of the smaller gold roses rectangle at the
back. Use foam tape to attach the rectangles to the card front as shown.

5 Cut a ⅞"x⅜" rectangle of gold. With the black pen, write "Happy Birthday". Punch a hole at one end; insert thread
through the hole, pull the ends together and tape them behind the top package as shown. Attach a small piece of foam
tape to the back of the rectangle and adhere it at an angle on the package.

Diamond Folds

Diamond folds lend sophisticated style to a card by adding geometric shapes and texture. Precise cutting is a must, so we've designed a tool to make it easy for you to create your own diamond folds. This special template features 14 favorite designs. In fact, we love using diamond cuts so much, we've added extra cards featuring this method! So, get your X-acto® knife ready—you'll need it to make these lovely cuts, and prepare to fold a new design technique into your paper crafting repetoire.

by Susan Cobb

Susan's Tip: Post-It® notes are great for holding the paper pieces in place while tracing and cutting the diamond fold cuts. Just place it at each corner to hold the paper to the cutting surface.

card inside

- *5"x6½" Paper Flair™ ivory blank card*
- *Paper Flair™ Teal Petite Prints™ Paper Pack*
- *Paper Flair™ Pastel Vellum Paper Pack*
- *solid ivory paper*
- *Paper Flair™ Diamond Folds Template*
- *silver pen (Sakura® Gelly Roll™)*
- *foam adhesive tape*
- *X-acto® knife, cutting surface*

1 Turn the card so the fold is on the right side. (Yes, right side!) Cut a 4¾"x6¼" rectangle from teal/ivory floral paper and glue it centered on the card front.

2 Cut a 3½"x6½" piece of ivory paper and score ½" along one long side. Glue the scored edge to the left side of the card back (on the opening side), creating a flap which overlaps onto the card front. Cut a 2⅞"x6¼" piece of dark teal striped paper and glue it to the ivory flap front, even with the left side.

3 Cut a 1¾"x5" rectangle from light teal striped paper and outline the edges in silver. Mat it on teal vellum, leaving a ¼" border. Place the rectangle on your cutting surface. Use the diamond cuts template (the design in the lower right corner) to draw the design on the center of the rectangle, beginning with the point of the first cut ¼" from the top edge of the striped paper. Use your ruler and X-acto® knife to carefully cut the design through both layers of the teal stripes and vellum. Fold down both layers of the first "V" cut. Repeat for every other strip and glue them in place. Glue the rectangle centered on the front flap.

4 Cut out two flowers from the remaining teal floral paper and mat each on ivory, leaving a very thin border. Adhere them to the diamond cut design with foam adhesive tape placed as shown. Cut a 1¾"x1⅛" piece of pastel teal vellum. With the silver pen, write "Thinking of You" on the vellum center, then outline the edges and add pen work to each end. Mat it on ivory, leaving a 1/16" border. Glue the tiny card to the front flap, carefully tucking it between the layers as shown.

by Susan Cobb

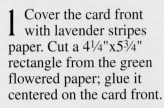

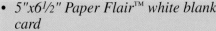

1 Cover the card front with lavender stripes paper. Cut a 4¼"x5¾" rectangle from the green flowered paper; glue it centered on the card front.

2 Cut a 3½" square each from the lavender leaves and solid lavender papers; glue them together back-to-back. Trace and transfer the pattern onto the leaves side. Use the X-acto® knife to cut out each "V" and the center heart; carefully fold the triangles forward and glue in place. Cut out a bouquet of flowers from the green flowered paper in a 1¼" square and glue behind the open heart window.

3 Glue a photo corner to each corner of the leaves square; then mat it on lavender, leaving a ³⁄₁₆" border. Glue it centered to the card front. With the white pen, write "Thank You" centered at the bottom of the leaves square.

- 5"x6½" Paper Flair™ white blank card
- Paper Flair™ Soft Patterns Paper Pack
- solid white paper
- white pen (Pentel Milky Gel Roller)
- 4 green photo corners (Canson-Talens)
- X-acto® knife, cutting surface
- tracing paper, transfer paper

- 5"x6½" Paper Flair™ ivory blank card
- Paper Flair™ Pink Petite Prints™ Paper Pack
- Paper Flair™ Pastel Vellum Paper Pack
- optional: Paper Flair™ Windows #1 Template
- Paper Flair™ Diamond Folds Template
- silver pen (Sakura® Gelly Roll™)
- foam adhesive tape
- X-acto® knife, cutting surface

card inside

by Susan Cobb

1 Cut a 4¾"x6⁵⁄₁₆" rectangle from the pansies paper, and glue it centered on the card front. Open card and place it face up on a cutting surface. Use the template to draw a 2¾" square in the upper center of the card front. With your ruler and X-acto® knife, carefully cut out the square.

2 Cut a 5½"x6½" piece of dark pink dotted paper and lay over the inside back of the card. Fold the excess ½" over the right side of the card back and glue the folded edge in place, to create a flap. Cut two 2" squares from the light pink striped and the light pink dotted papers. Place the squares with alternate patterns together in the center of the dark pink dotted flap, making sure the center of the four squares is centered in the window. Glue the squares in place.

3 Cut a 3½" square from pastel pink vellum. Use the template and pencil to lightly draw the diamond cuts oval on the center of the vellum. Place the vellum on a cutting surface and with your X-acto® knife, carefully cut each "V" and fold each back. (Tip: Carefully creasing with your fingernail helps the folds to lay flat without gluing.) Glue the vellum square to the center of the four squares, with the oval centered through the window.

4 Cut out a pansy cluster, outline it with the silver pen and adhere it with foam tape to the card as shown. Outline the folds of the diamond cuts, the edge of the window and the outer edge of the four squares with the silver pen.

Diamond Folds

by Lisa Garcia-Bergstedt

- 5"x6½" Paper Flair™ white blank card
- Paper Flair™ Purple Petite Prints™ Paper Pack
- Paper Flair™ Windows #2 Template
- Paper Flair™ Diamond Folds Template
- white pen (Sakura® Gelly Roll™)
- 14" of ⅛" wide lavender satin ribbon (Offray®)
- mini glue dots (Glue Dots, Inc.)
- X-acto® knife, cutting surface

1 Cut the card to 5" square. Cover the inside back with lavender stars paper. Cut a 4¾" square from the purple stripes paper and glue it centered on the card front.

2 Use the star template to draw a 2½" wide star on the center of the card front. Place the diamond folds "plus sign" design centered along the left side of the stripes; use your pencil to draw the design onto the card. Place the card opened face up on a cutting surface. Use the X-acto® knife to cut out star and plus signs.

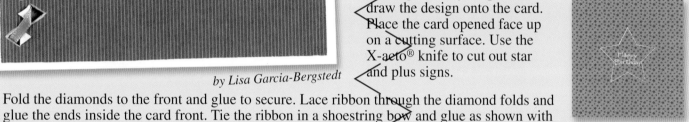

diamond fold pattern

card inside

3 Fold the diamonds to the front and glue to secure. Lace ribbon through the diamond folds and glue the ends inside the card front. Tie the ribbon in a shoestring bow and glue as shown with a glue dot. With the white pen, outline the diamond folds and star; then trace the shape of the star onto the inside back and write "Happy Birthday".

- 5"x6½" Paper Flair™ white blank card
- Paper Flair™ Purple & Blue Paper Pack
- solid papers: black, white
- X-acto® knife, cutting surface

1 Cover the card front with black paper. Cut a 4¾"x6½" rectangle of the blue with stitches paper. Glue it centered on the card front, leaving a ⅛" border on the left and right sides.

2 Cut out a 6½" long rectangle from the blue diamonds paper, making sure there are 7 full columns of dark blue diamonds with full diamonds at the top and bottom of the rectangle. Place it on a cutting surface and with the X-acto® knife cut along the top half of the center top diamond (fourth from left side) and top half of the lavender diamond on either side (it should measure ½"). Skip the next diamond row below and repeat the cutting process to make seven full cuts. Fold each triangle down to reveal the white background, forming a diamond.

3 Cut a 2½"x6½" rectangle of black paper. Glue the diamond paper on the black, ⅛" from the left side. With the X-acto® knife, cut a triangle inside the top diamond fold, leaving a ¹⁄₁₆" black border on the upper sides of each hole. Repeat for each of the diamond cut-outs.

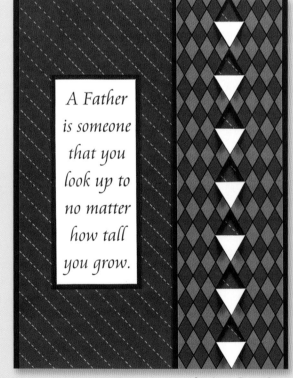

by Amy Gustafson

4 Fold under ⅜" on the right side of the diamond mat, leaving a ⅛" black border along the right edge. Glue the folded portion to the card back so that the diamond section wraps to the card front. Print out or write your message on a 1½"x3½" rectangle of white paper, mat it on black, leaving a ⅛" border. Glue it to the card front as shown.

- *5"x6½" Paper Flair™ white blank card*
- *Paper Flair™ Purple & Blue Paper Pack*
- *Paper Flair™ Blossoms & Buds Paper Pack*
- *Paper Flair™ Laser Motifs Card Embellishments*
- *solid lavender paper*
- *silver pen (Zebra Jimmie Gel Rollerball)*
- *X-acto® knife, cutting surface*
- *tracing paper, transfer paper*

card inside

1 Trim 1" off the open edge of card front. Cover the front with lavender paper. Cut a 3¾"x6¼" rectangle of purple hydrangeas paper and glue it centered on the card front. Trace and transfer the heart from the laser motif onto lavender and cut it out. Cut out the laser heart motif with the filigree frame. Glue the lavender heart behind the laser heart, then glue it centered on the card front. Cut two ¼"x2¾" strips of purple moiré paper and glue to top and bottom edges of the motif.

2 Cover the inside back with purple moiré paper. Cut a ¾"x5" strip of purple moire paper, then mat on lavender, leaving a ⅛" border. Place the small "V" shapes pattern centered on the strip; use a pencil to draw them onto the strip. Place the strip on a cutting surface and cut out the "V" shapes. Fold down the triangles and glue them in place. Glue the diamond cuts strip to the inside back, along the right side.

3 Use the silver pen to outline the diamond cuts and ¼" moiré strips.

by Susan Cobb

diamond fold pattern

- *5"x6½" Paper Flair™ white blank card*
- *Paper Flair™ Blossoms & Buds Paper Pack*
- *Paper Flair™ Gold Patterns Paper Pack*
- *solid pale yellow paper*
- *9" of 5/16" wide black sheer ribbon with satin edges (Offray®)*
- *X-acto® knife, cutting surface*
- *tracing paper, transfer paper*

card front

1 Cover card front with red roses paper. Cut a 3"x7" piece of pale yellow paper and a 2"x7" piece of gold paper. Glue the gold centered on the yellow. Place the small "V" shapes pattern centered on the gold; use a pencil to draw six "V" onto the gold. Place it on a cutting surface and cut on the lines. Fold the triangles forward and glue them in place.

2 Fold ½" under along the top of the gold diamond strip and glue it to the center top back of the card, so the flap wraps to the front. Cut a 3¾"x5" piece of red roses paper to make a bottom flap, trimming along the roses on the top 5" long side. Mat on gold paper and leave a thin edge next to the trimmed edge. Fold ½" under along the bottom, and glue the flap to the bottom of card back, so it wraps to the front.

3 Use the ribbon to make a shoestring bow with 1¼" long loops and glue it to the upper edge of the red roses flap.

by Susan Cobb

diamond fold pattern

by Amy Gustafson

- *two 5"x6½" Paper Flair™ white blank cards*
- *Paper Flair™ Burgundy & Rose Paper Pack*
- *solid white paper*
- *Paper Flair™ Painted Vellum Card Embellishments*
- *X-acto® knife, cutting surface*

1 Cut out a 4¾"x6¼" rectangle of pink with stitches; glue it centered to the front of the first card (card A). Place the second card (card B) open and face down on a cutting surface; score a vertical line 2½" from each side, but do not fold yet.

2 Cut a 4¾"x6¼" rectangle of the pink diamonds paper; glue it to the first and second panels of card B, leaving a ⅛" white border along the edges. Cut out a 4¾"x6¼" rectangle of pink swirls; glue it to the third and fourth panels, leaving a ⅛" white border along each edge.

3 Place card A opened face down on a cutting surface; place card B directly on top face up with all edges even. Cut out the "Just For You" vellum motif and place it on card B centered on the first scored line 1" from the top edge. Lightly outline only the left half of the motif in pencil; then remove the motif. With an X-acto® knife, cut along the pencil lines through both cards on the first panel, making sure not to cut beyond the scored line. Remove card B. With a ruler, use the X-acto® knife to cut out the right side of the 3-edged window on card A.

4 With card A still face down, place card B directly on top face up, making sure the edges are even (the cutout piece on card B should insert directly into the window of card A). Glue the first panel sections together and the fourth side panels together, leaving the two inner panels unattached.

5 With the card open, glue the vellum motif to the window cutout with half of it extending onto the second inside panel. Close the card; glue ⅛" wide strips of white paper around the window edges for a frame.

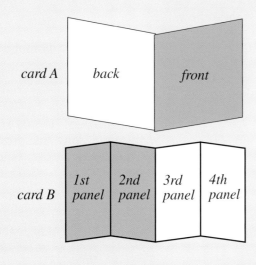

card A — back — front

card B — 1st panel — 2nd panel — 3rd panel — 4th panel

inside card

- *two 5"x6½" Paper Flair™ white blank cards*
- *Paper Flair™ Pink Petite Prints™ Paper Pack*
- *Paper Flair™ Embossed Motifs Card Embellishments*
- *optional: Paper Flair™ Windows #1 Template*
- *solid papers: pale yellow, white*
- *24" of ⅛" wide ivory satin ribbon (Offray)*
- *⅛" wide circle punch (Marvy® Uchida)*
- *X-acto® knife, cutting surface*

1 Trim 1½" off the front side edge of one card. Trim 1" off the front of the second card and ½" off the back side edge.

2 Cover the first card front with floral stripes paper and the inside back with the pansies paper. Cover the second card front with pink dots and the inside back with the pansies paper. Cut ¾"x6½" strips of the floral stripes and pink dots papers. Glue the floral stripes strip at the right edge of the second card inside back; glue the pink dots strip to the right edge of the first card inside back.

3 Use the template to trace three 1½" squares on the front of the first card, angled as shown. Open the first card face up on a cutting surface. Use the X-acto® knife to cut out each square. Close the first card and insert the second card inside it, so the right edges appear in tiers. Use a pencil to trace the squares onto the second layer. Open the second card face up on a cutting surface. Cut out the top and bottom squares only. Reinsert this card inside the first card and trace the two squares onto the third layer. Remove the second card and cut out the top square only. Reinsert the card inside the first card and trace the top square onto the fourth layer.

by Amy Gustafson

4 Cut three embossed motifs into 1½" squares; glue onto yellow and tear, leaving ⅛" mats. Glue a motif to each traced square on the card layers. Tear strips of yellow paper, then trim the right side straight to make each ³⁄₁₆" wide. Glue around each window and along the right edges of the four layers. Punch a hole in the center folds 1" from the top and bottom edges. Thread the ribbon through the holes to the outside and tie it in a shoestring bow to secure. Cut squares and rectangles of white, mat each on yellow and glue as shown for journaling.

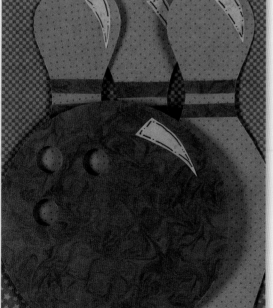

1 Glue the cards, one inside of the other, forming a flap on the left and one on the right. Glue the blue/purple checked paper to the inside back.
Cut out the three pins and the ball. Glue two pins side-by-side on the right flap, with one pin next to the center fold. Use the X-acto® knife to cut out the pin shapes.

- *two 5"x6½" Paper Flair™ white blank cards*
- *patterned papers in this book*
- *black pen (Sakura® Gelly Roll™)*
- *X-acto® knife, cutting surface*

2 Glue the bowling ball on the left flap even with the side fold. Use the X-acto® knife to cut out the ball shape and finger holes.

3 Cut out the stripes and highlights; glue them to the pins. Cut out the pocket and glue the sides and bottom to the inside back, creating a pocket. Cut out the greeting and glue it to the single pin, then slip it inside the pocket.

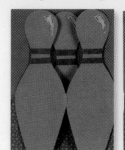

flap opened   *inside card*

by Lisa Garcia-Bergstedt

Double Fold-Backs

by Lisa Garcia-Bergstedt

- two 5"x6½" Paper Flair™ white blank cards
- Paper Flair™ Soft Patterns Paper Pack
- Paper Flair™ Pastel Vellum Paper Pack
- solid white paper
- beads: three ¼" pearl white hearts, one ¼" green star, eight ⅜" white bugle beads
- 60 yellow, green and purple seed beads
- black pen (Zig® Millenium)
- mini glue dots (Glue Dots, Inc.)
- 6" of .5mm jewelry cord (Stretch Magic), metal crimp
- X-acto® knife, cutting surface
- tracing paper, transfer paper

1 Open each card and place the left side of one over the right side of the other; glue the halves together. Turn the card over and use the blunt edge of the X-acto® knife to vertically score down the center of each side; then fold each flap back to the outside folds.

2 Cut two 2½"x6½" rectangles each of green dotted and lavender striped papers. Glue a dotted piece to each outer half; then open the card and glue a striped piece to each inner half of the fronts. Cut a 5"x6½" rectangle of purple leaves and glue it to the middle section of the card.

3 Trace the circle pattern. Close the card and transfer the circle to the center of the front flaps. Open the card and finish drawing each circle on the striped sections. Place the card on a cutting surface and cut on the line on the striped halves only of each circle. Cut two 3" circles of lavender flowers on yellow and mat each on lavender vellum, leaving a ⅛" border. Glue a floral circle to each drawn circle on the card. Use the large heart pattern to cut two hearts of lavender vellum and mat each on white, leaving a 1/16" border. Glue a heart centered on each floral circle.

4 Cut out one 1½" and one 1" square of white. Cut each square in half diagonally, then mat each on lavender vellum, leaving a 1/16" border. Cut out four flower motifs and glue one to each triangle. Glue the triangles to the card corners as shown.

5 Cut a third 3" circle from the floral paper, mat it on lavender vellum, then on the dots paper and again on lavender vellum, each with a ⅛" border. Glue it centered on the inside middle section of the card. Use the small heart pattern to cut a heart of lavender vellum, mat it on white, leaving a 1/16" border and glue it centered on the middle floral circle. Use the pattern below to cut a lavender vellum sign and glue it over the heart. Cut a 2⅞"x½" rectangle of lavender vellum and glue it below the middle circle. Write on the vellums.

6 **For the bracelet:** Thread the jewelry cord in the following bead combination: one heart, one yellow seed bead, one bugle bead and fourteen seed beads; then repeat three times, using the green heart in the fourth bead combination. Crimp the ends together to secure.

card inside

- 5"x6½" Paper Flair™ white blank card
- Paper Flair™ Purple & Blue Paper Pack
- Paper Flair™ Windows #2 Template
- solid lavender paper
- X-acto® knife, cutting surface

card inside

1½" long cut →

1 Cover the card front, inside front and inside back with lavender paper. Open the card face up on a cutting surface. On the front, cut out a 2" wide by 3¼" tall piece from the upper right corner. Use the dull edge of the X-acto® knife to score 1½" from the right edge of each half section; then cut 1½" as shown above.

2 Cut 4¾"x6¼" and 3⅛"x2⅞" rectangles from blue/lavender diamonds. Glue the large rectangle centered on the inside back and the small rectangle on the card front lower section, centered between the side fold and scored line. Cut two 1⅜"x3" rectangles of lavender stars on blue. With the card open face down, glue a stars rectangle centered on each outer flap of the two scored sections.

3 Use the template to draw a star centered on the scored line of each section. Cut out only the right side of each star, so when the scored section is folded back the right side of each star extends outward. Cut two stars of lavender swirls paper, mat each on lavender and cut with an ⅛" border. Glue one to the inside front of each star. Cut out 1¼"x1½", 1⅛"x1⅛" and 3"x½" rectangles of white, mat each on lavender and cut with an ⅛" border. Glue them to the card as shown for your message.

by Amy Gustafson

by Amy Gustafson

1 Cut both cards to 5" squares. Open one card face up on a cutting surface, so the card front is to your right side. Use the dull edge of the X-acto® knife to score a line 2½" from the right edge of the card front, so when it is closed the front panel folds to the left. Repeat the process for the second card.

- two 5"x6½" Paper Flair™ white blank cards
- patterned papers in this book
- pink pen (Sakura® Permapaque™)
- X-acto® knife, cutting surface

2 Cut out the patterned paper shapes. Glue the rectangle with the pink diamonds heart to the inside back of the first card, next to the center fold. Cut the excess inside back off, cutting along the right side of the rectangle and heart edge. Open both cards inside up and glue the back side of the burgundy suede rectangle to the front flap of the second card, forming accordian folds with the two cards.

3 With the card fully open, glue the burgundy heart rectangle to the leftmost panel. Place the card on a cutting surface. Use the X-acto® knife to cut along the right side only of the heart. Glue the 5" burgundy suede square to the inside back of the card.

4 Cut four ³⁄₁₆" wide stitched pink strips; cut three to 5" lengths and four to 2½" lengths. Glue the strips ⅛" from the top and bottom edges, with two 5" strips on the inside back and the shorter strips on the two heart panels. Tie a knot in the last strip and glue to the burgundy heart. Use the pink pen to write "I Love You" on the inside back.

card inside

Flaps

Making cards with flaps adds an extra flair to your paper crafting. Notice on these pages how each card uses not just one flap, but several!

by Susan Cobb

top flap open   card inside

1 Cover the card front with yellow floral paper. Transfer the front flap pattern (see page 77) onto the card front. Cut along the top portion; mat the top portion only on white, leaving a 1/16" border. Cut a 2 3/8" square from the green dotted paper; mat it on white, leaving a 1/16" border. Glue it to the center section of the card front even with the cut edge. Open the card face up on a cutting surface; measure, mark and cut out a 1 1/2" square window from the center of the matted square.

2 Transfer the inner flap pattern onto the purple leaves paper; mat only the top portion on white, leaving a 1/16" border. Fold 1/2" under on the right edge. Glue the folded edge to the card back on the right side so the flap wraps inside the card. Close the front and use a pencil to lightly draw the window onto the inner flap. Open it on a cutting surface and cut out the window.

3 Cover the inside back with the lavender/purple stripes paper. Cut out a 1 3/4"x1 5/8" rectangle from the yellow floral paper with a bouquet in the center. Mat it on green dotted paper, leaving a 1/8" border; mat it again on white, leaving a 1/16" border. Glue it to the inside card back showing through the windows.

4 With the white pen, write "My heart fills with love" above the roses mat on the inside back and "Whenever I think of you" below. Tie a shoestring bow with 1/2" loops and glue to the card front.

- 5"x6 1/2" Paper Flair™ white blank card
- Paper Flair™ Soft Patterns Paper Pack
- solid white paper
- optional: Paper Flair™ Windows #1 Template
- white pen (Pentel Milky Gel Roller)
- 9" of 3/8" wide lavender satin ribbon (Offray®)
- X-acto® knife, cutting surface
- mini glue dots (Glue Dots Inc.)

- 5"x6 1/2" Paper Flair™ ivory blank card
- Paper Flair™ White, Cream & Laser Lace Petite Prints™ Paper Pack
- solid pale yellow paper
- X-acto® knife, cutting surface
- tracing paper, transfer paper

1 Open the card face down on a cutting surface. Use the dull edge of the X-acto® knife to vertically score the front 2 1/2" from the edges; fold the sides in to meet at the center front. Measure 2 3/16" from the top edge on the left side flap and cut from the right edge to the fold. Repeat 2 3/16" below the first cut, then measure and cut the right flap to match it. Open all the flaps and glue a 4 7/8"x6 3/8" rectangle of tan swirls centered on the inside back.

2 Cover three front panels with tan dots paper as shown. Cut three 1 1/2" pale yellow squares and glue one to each tan dots paper, angled as shown. Trace and transfer the letters onto the tan/ivory diamonds; cut out and glue to each ivory square. Tear one oval shape each from the ivory hollow dots, herringbone and tan mosaic papers; two sets of ears and noses from tan dots; a nose and inner ears from pale yellow and outer ears from herringbone. Assemble into dogs as shown and glue to the ivory panels.

3 Print out or write your messages on rectangles of pale yellow and glue them to the inside back centered under a panel as shown.

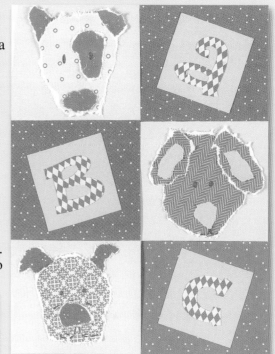

by Lisa Garcia-Bergstedt

card inside

28

Flaps

- 5"x6½" Paper Flair™ white blank card
- Paper Flair™ Blossoms & Buds Paper Pack
- Paper Flair™ Purple & Blue Paper Pack
- solid purple paper
- black pen (Sakura® Gelly Roll™)
- 8" of ⅝" wide lavender satin ribbon (Offray®)
- tracing paper, transfer paper

1 Cut the card to 5" square; then cut the card in half along the fold line. Set aside one piece.

2 Trace the flap pattern (see page 79); transfer it twice onto the purple hydrangeas paper and twice onto the purple sponged paper. Cut them out and mat each on purple paper, leaving a ¹⁄₁₆" border. Fold each along the ½" line and glue the hydrangeas flap to the top back of the card, with the patterned side folding onto the card front. Repeat this process with one of the sponged paper flaps on the left side of the card; the second hydrangeas flap on the bottom and the second sponged flap on the right.

3 Tie the ribbon into a shoestring bow with 1" loops. Glue it centered to the bottom edge of the top hydrangeas flap. With the top flap folded down, fold over the left flap, then the bottom flap, and then the right flap over. Tuck the edges of the flaps under the ribbon and the top edge of the right flap under the top flap. With the black pen, write "Wishing you" and "a happy birthday!" as shown.

by Amy Gustafson

- two 5"x6½" Paper Flair™ white blank cards
- Paper Flair™ White, Cream & Laser Lace Petite Prints™ Paper Pack
- solid papers: brown, white
- black pen (Sakura® 3mm Micron)
- 10" of twine
- mini scallop decorative scissors (Fiskars®)
- glue dot (Glue Dots Inc.)
- ¾" wide black button

1 With the fold on the left, trim 2¾" off the top of the first card. Cut a 3" length of twine, make a loop and tape the ends centered on the right edge of the card back. Cover the card front and back with tan flecks paper and the entire inside with ivory mosaic. Cut a 1½"x3¾" rectangle of brown, trimming the long sides with decorative scissors. Glue it to the outside fold so it evenly wraps to each side.

2 Open the cut off piece of the card and cover it with ivory swirls, then trim along the top with decorative scissors. Glue the sides and bottom to the inside of the card.

3 With the fold on the left, trim off 2½" off the top of the second card. Cover the inside with tan tri-dots, then trim along the top with decorative scissors. Glue the sides and bottom to the inside of the card.

4 With the remaining second card portion, place the fold on top and trim 3¾" off the bottom. Cut a half circle out of the bottom front only. Cover the front card with tan tri-dots. Glue inside the card as shown. Write your message on rectangles of white; mat each on brown, leaving a ⅛" border. Glue inside the card as shown. Draw stitch marks along the inside and outside edges of the card. Thread and tie twine into the button holes. Close the card and place a glue dot on the outside right, centered across the loop, then place the button on top and wrap the loop around it.

by Lisa Garcia-Bergstedt

card inside

inside with open flap

29

Fold-Backs

Fold-backs add an interesting twist to cards by providing a special section that is literally folded back onto itself. Of course, we had to design some with flair, as you see here and on the next page. Amy begins with an elegant design in soft pinks. Lisa shows how a touch of whimsey always make cards fun with her rendition of a cat. Amy concludes the section with an invitation that's sure to kept well after the party. So, go ahead—it's easy!

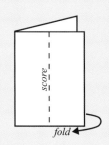

score

fold

by Amy Gustafson

- *5"x6½" Paper Flair™ white blank card*
- *Paper Flair™ Pink Petite Prints™ Paper Pack*
- *Paper Flair™ Painted Vellum Card Embellishments*
- *solid white paper*
- *X-acto® knife, cutting surface*

1 Open the card and place it face down on a cutting surface. Use the dull edge of the X-acto® knife to score 2½" along the card front, so the right end folds back onto the front.

2 Cut a 2¼"x6¼" rectangle of pink swirls. Glue it to the front flap, even with the scored fold, leaving a ⅛" white border along each open edge.

3 Cut out the pink roses vellum heart. Mat it on pink stripes, leaving a ⅛" border; then mat it again on white, leaving a ⅛" border. Open the card inside up, with the swirls paper at the top. Glue the heart centered on the top of the fold back score line, with half of it extending beyond the scored line. Place the open card on a cutting surface. Use the X-acto® knife to cut out the bottom heart shape along the white mat, without cutting beyond the scored line as shown. Refold the card, keeping the point of the heart unfolded.

4 Cut a 4⅞"x6¼" rectangle from the pink mosaic paper. Glue it centered on the inside back, with the paper next to the fold creating a white border along the three open edges. Cut a 6¹⁄₁₆"x¼" strip of pink swirls; mat it on white, leaving a ¹⁄₁₆" border. Glue the strip ⅜" from the pink mosaic edge.

card inside

KNOWING THE SCORE: To get clean score lines, we suggest placing a ruler up against the line you wish to score. Besides using the dull edge of an X-acto® knife, you can also use a stylus. Be sure to keep the line perfectly straight and apply the score to the side of the card you wish to fold inward.

- *5"x6½" Paper Flair™ white blank card*
- *patterned papers in this book*
- *solid white paper*
- *black pen (Sakura® 3mm Micron)*
- *X-acto® knife, cutting surface*

1 Open the card face down on a cutting surface. Use the dull edge of the X-acto® knife to vertically score down the center of the card front, fold the front back onto itself.

2 Cut out the papers and shapes for the card in this book. Cover the inside front and inside back with the lavender dots on blue paper. Mat the 1⅛"x3" rectangle of green floral paper on white, leaving a ⅛" border along the top, bottom and left sides. Glue the lavender striped cat to the rectangle, aligning the center point between the ears with the left edge of the rectangle.

3 With the card open, glue the rectangle on the inside front right edge, even with the scored line. Place the open card on a cutting surface. Use the knife to cut out the right half of the cat shape, without cutting beyond the scored line. Refold the card keeping the cat flat.

4 Glue the message square centered on the green floral rectangle; then mat the floral rectangle on white, leaving a ⅛" border. Glue it centered to the inside back, aligning it with the cat rectangle when closed. Use the black pen to draw whiskers and stitch marks for the cat's mouth and a border around the rectangle, message square and the lines around the cat.

card inside

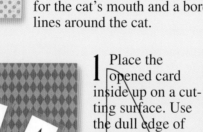

by Lisa Garcia-Bergstedt

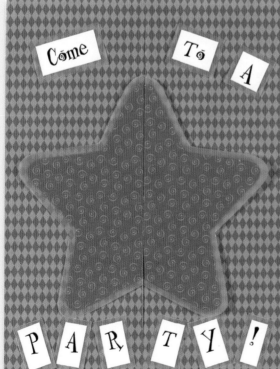

by Amy Gustafson

1 Place the opened card inside up on a cutting surface. Use the dull edge of the X-acto® knife to vertically score down the center front and center back. Fold the edges of card in toward the center.

- *5"x6½" Paper Flair™ white blank card*
- *Paper Flair™ Teal Petite Prints™ Paper Pack*
- *Paper Flair™ Pastel Vellum Paper Pack*
- *solid white paper*
- *Paper Flair™ Card Fold-Backs Template*
- *X-acto® knife, cutting surface*

2 Place the straight edge of the half-star template ½" from the left edge of the dark teal swirls paper. Use a pencil to draw the star shape; cut it out with the ½" extension. Flip the template over and repeat adding a ½" on the right edge of the half star. Mat each half-star on teal vellum, leaving a ⅛" border along the shaped sides. Fold ½" under on the extension edges. Glue only the extension of each centered on the panel open edges, so the patterned sides of the star pieces fold over the front.

3 Lift the star shape and cover each front panel with teal diamonds, covering the extensions. Open the card and cover the inside back with the light teal with dots paper.

4 Print out lettering on white rectangles and squares; mat each on teal vellum, then arrange them on the card front and inside as shown.

card inside

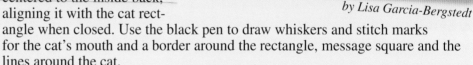

31

Hinges

by Amy Gustafson

- *5"x6½" Paper Flair™ white blank card*
- *Paper Flair™ Blossoms & Buds Paper Pack*
- *Paper Flair™ Gold Patterns Paper Pack*
- *solid purple paper*
- *gold pen (Sakura® Gelly Roll™)*
- *14" of ⅝" wide lavender satin ribbon*
- *X-acto® knife, cutting surface*
- *tracing paper, transfer paper*

1 Cut the card in half along the fold. Score a line 1¾" from the short edge of one piece for the card front; fold along the line and glue the 1¾" section to the back left side of the other card piece, with the flap wrapping to the front.

2 Cover the front flap with gold paper. Cut a 4¾" square from the hydrangeas paper; glue it even with the left side, leaving a ⅛" border on the top and bottom edges.

3 Trace and transfer the flap pattern on page 78 onto purple paper. Mat it on gold, leaving a ⅛" border. Fold under 1" as shown on the pattern; glue this section to the right side back of the card, with the flap wrapping to the front. Glue ribbon vertically centered on the right flap. Tie a shoestring bow with 1" loops and glue it centered on the flap.

4 Open the card face up on a cutting surface. With the X-acto® knife, cut a 1⅛" long slit on the large front flap, centered ⁹⁄₁₆" from the right side edge. Use the knife to carefully cut 1⅛" length around the outline of some petals in the lower left corner of the front flap. Cut a 1¼"x1¾" rectangle of purple; mat it on gold, leaving a ⅛" border. With the gold pen, write "Thinking of You"; insert it as shown and glue.

- *5"x6½" Paper Flair™ white blank card*
- *patterned papers in this book*
- *solid white paper*
- *black pen (Sakura® 3mm Micron)*
- *X-acto® knife, cutting surface*

1 Open the card and place it inside up on a cutting surface. Use the dull edge of the X-acto® knife to vertically score down the center front and center back. Fold each panel toward the center.

2 Cut out the patterned papers for this card. Place the fingers on each side panel as shown. Cut out the finger shapes. Mat the pink swirls rectangle on white, leaving a ⅟₁₆" border along the top, bottom and left sides. Glue it face up to the back of the fingers on your left. Place the left panel on a cutting surface and cut out the tip of the first finger only.

3 Mat the rectangle with the heart on white, leaving a ⅟₁₆" border. Glue it to the back of the fingers as shown.

4 Open the card and cover the inside center back with pink mesh. With the black pen, write "Happy Anniversary!!" and "I love you!" as shown. Close the card and tuck the left side of the heart under the left finger. Use the pen to write "for you" on the heart. Draw stitch marks around the heart and rectangles.

by Lisa Garcia-Bergstedt

card inside

32

- *5"x6½" Paper Flair™ white blank card*
- *Paper Flair™ Blue Petite Prints™ Paper Pack*
- *solid papers: yellow, white*
- *18" of ¼" wide white satin ribbon (Offray®)*

card front with hinge open

1 Cut a 4⅞"x6⅜" rectangle from the light blue dots paper; glue it centered on the card front. Cut a 4¼"x5¾" rectangle from the blue herringbone; glue it centered on the card front.

2 Cut a 3"x6½" rectangle from the blue floral paper; glue it on white, trimming the edges even. Cut around the flowers along the left long side; then fold ½" under on the right side Glue the folded section to the right side of the card back, so the flowers wrap to the front. Glue the ribbon around the floral flap and tie a shoestring bow with ½" loops near the top and glue it in place.

3 Print or write your messages on 2"x1½" and 1¾"x1 1/16" rectangles of white; mat each on yellow, leaving a 1/16" border. Glue them to the card front as shown. Cut out four different flower clusters from the blue floral paper and glue to the card front as shown.

by Amy Gustafson

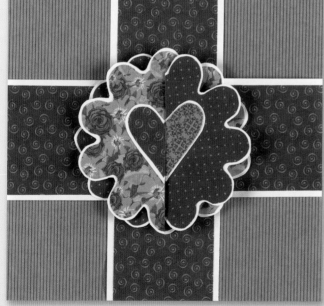

by Lisa Garcia-Bergstedt

card front with flaps opened

- *5"x6½" Paper Flair™ white blank card*
- *Paper Flair™ Purple Petite Prints™ Paper Pack*
- *solid white paper*
- *tracing paper, transfer paper*

1 Cut the card to 5" square. Cover the card front with lavender stripes. Cut a 1½"x5" rectangle from the purple swirls paper; mat it on white, leaving a ⅛" border only on the long sides. Glue the swirls centered on the card front as shown above.

2 Trace and transfer the heart onto the purple swirls and the lavender mosaic; cut out and mat each on white, leaving a 1/16" border. Trace and transfer a flower shape onto purple dots and purple roses papers; cut out and mat each on white, leaving a 1/16" border. Glue the mosaic heart centered on the purple dots flower. Turn the purple roses flower slightly and glue the swirls heart centered on it. Make a slit from the bottom of purple roses flower to the center top point of the swirls heart. Cut a slit from the top of the purple dots flower to the bottom point of the mosaic heart.

3 Cut two 2½"x1½" rectangles of purple swirls. Mat each on white, leaving a ⅛" border on each long side and ½" border on one short side of each. Fold the ½" borders under and glue each centered on a side back of the card so the patterned ends meet at the center.

4 Glue the purple dots flower to the left swirls hinge with the slit even with its right edge. Glue the purple rose flower to the right side hinge, with the slit even with its left edge. Slide the two flowers together through the slits.

Just like you might slip on a jacket, you'll notice these card jackets slip right over the card. Vellum jackets offer some lovely translucent effects.

by Shauna Berglund-Immel

card front without the jacket

- 5"x6½" Paper Flair™ white blank card
- Paper Flair™ Blossoms & Buds Paper Pack
- Paper Flair™ Pastel Vellum Paper Pack
- Paper Flair™ Silver Patterns Paper Pack
- solid white paper
- silver pen (Pentel Hybrid Gel Roller)
- black pen (Sakura® Gelly Roll™)
- 2" of silver thread
- X-acto® knife, cutting surface
- foam adhesive tape

1 Cut the card so it's 4½"x6½". Cut a 4"x5⅞" rectangle from the lavender flowers paper; mat it on silver, leaving a ⅛" border. Glue it centered on the card front.

2 From the remaining lavender flowers paper, cut out eight individual flowers. From the white daisies paper, cut out 11 daisies; then cut out 11 ivy leaves from the ivy paper. Glue four ivy leaves to form a 2" square centered on the card front. Glue three diasies on top, overlapping; glue four purple flowers evenly spaced on top. Cut a 1⅛"x½" rectangle of white. Use the silver pen to outline it and use the black pen to write "For You" on the tag. Fold the thread in a loop and glue the ends to the back of the tag, the loop to the lower daisy and the tag as shown.

3 Place the 5⅝"x11" rectangle of blue vellum flat; score a line 4½" from the right end and another 1¾" from the left end; fold each panel inward. Turn the vellum over and glue one daisy centered on the 4½"x5⅝" section. Glue the other cut flowers along the left edge, beginning with the ivy, then four daisies. Use foam tape to attach the other flowers as shown. Place the card in the center vellum section, add a touch of glue to the center back of the card to secure it; wrap the panels to the front.

- 5"x6½" Paper Flair™ white blank card
- Paper Flair™ Soft Patterns Paper Pack
- Paper Flair™ Vellum Paper Pack
- blue glitter pen (Sakura® Gelly Roll™)
- 9" of ¼" wide lavender satin ribbon (Offray®)
- X-acto® knife, cutting surface
- tracing paper, transfer paper

card front without the jacket

by Susan Cobb

1 Cut the card to 5" square. Cover the card front with the purple plaid. Cut a 4½" square of lavender stripes; glue it centered on the card front.

2 Trim the pansies on vellum to 5"x11". Place it face down with the card centered on top; fold each side in to form the creases only. Remove the vellum, unfold it and place the left fold over the pattern and trace it. Turn the vellum over and repeat the pattern on the right fold. Trace a 1" square centered between the ovals. Place the vellum on a cutting surface. Use the X-acto® knife to cut out the oval halves and the square.

3 Refold the vellum and glue the back edges together. Use the pen to outline the oval halves and the square. Use the ribbon to make a shoestring bow with ¾" long loops. Glue the bow centered below the square on the vellum jacket. From the remaining vellum, cut out a pansy and glue it to the card front centered in the vellum window.

oval-half pattern

- *5"x6½" Paper Flair™ ivory blank card*
- *Paper Flair™ Blossoms & Buds Paper Pack*
- *Paper Flair™ Vellum Paper Pack*
- *Paper Flair™ Gold Patterns Paper Pack*
- *solid ivory paper*

1 Cut the card to a 5" square. Cut a 4¾" square from the roses paper; glue it centered on the card front.

2 Cut out a 10¾"x5¾" rectangle of the vellum dots paper. Place it horizontally and fold in 2½" on each end. Trace the triangle pattern on page 78; transfer it to each end of the vellum and cut the points. Turn the card with the fold at the top and place it centered on the vellum. Attach the vellum to the back of the card lightly gluing the center top and bottom.

3 From the rose paper, cut out a 1½" square centered on a rose. Mat it on gold, leaving a ⅛" border; mat again on pale yellow, leaving a ⅛" border. Turn it on point and glue a ¾" corner to the left vellum flap, making sure it is centered on the card front. Tuck the right jacket flap under the rose diamond.

card front without the jacket

by Susan Cobb

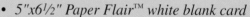

1 Cut a 4¾"x6¼" rectangle from purple moiré. Glue it centered on the card front. Cut a 2½"x3½" rectangle of purple/lavender checked; mat it

- *5"x6½" Paper Flair™ white blank card*
- *Paper Flair™ Purple & Blue Paper Pack*
- *Paper Flair™ Vellum Paper Pack*
- *Paper Flair™ Laser Words Card Embellishments*
- *solid white paper*
- *26" of ⅜" wide white sheer ribbon with satin edges (Offray®)*
- *white pen (Pentel Milky Gel Roller)*
- *X-acto® knife, cutting surface*

on white, leaving a 1/16" border. Cut the "just for you" laser motif into a 2 1/16"x3¼" rectangle. Then carefully cut out the message box and set it aside. Cut a 1½" square from purple/lavender diamonds and glue it behind the present in the laser motif. Glue the laser motif centered on the checked mat, then centered on the card front.

2 Cut a 4⅛"x5¾" rectangle of purple stars; glue it centered on the inside back. Glue the "just for you" laser motif centered on the stars.

3 Trim the short ends of the 5⅝"x11" lavender vellum diamonds around the diamond shapes. Use the white pen to outline the vellum edges. Place the vellum diamonds face down and the card on top, 2½" from the right edge; then fold in each vellum side to wrap around the card. Make creases along these folds.

4 Remove the card and make a ⅜" wide slit in the vellum centered on each fold line. With the vellum diamonds face down, thread the ribbon through the slits so it is on top of the vellum in the center section and under it on the sides. Place the card back in the center section of the vellum, gluing it at the center back to secure. Fold in the two vellum sides to overlap at the front, then tie the ribbon into a shoestring bow.

by Amy Gustafson

card front without the jacket

card inside

Laser Lace

Laser lace is so exquisite, we can't resist using it. It's actually cut with a beam of light! Only a laser could translate such delicate details into paper, yet retain its beauty even when folded. We've designed three simple, yet elegant cards to highlight this exciting product. As you can see, it enhances any design or technique. You'll be so amazed, you'll want to order a stack of it. (We, of course, offer it in single sheets or packages of 50 sheets. Plus, it's part of the first Paper Pack listed below.) So have fun with this wonderful paper!

by Amy Gustafson

- *5"x6½" Paper Flair™ ivory blank card*
- *patterned papers in this book*
- *Paper Flair™ White, Cream & Laser Lace Petite Prints™ Paper Pack*
- *X-acto® knife, cutting surface*

1 Cut the card to a 5" square. Cut out the patterned papers for this card in the book. Glue the tan tri-dots square centered on the card front. Open the card and place it face up on a cutting surface. Use the X-acto® knife to cut out the white areas.

2 Cut eight 1" squares from the laser lace. Fold each into a kite as shown below. Arrange the kites with the folds to the back and the narrow ends pointing to the center. Once arranged, glue the pieces in place.

3 Cut a 2½" square from the hollow dots paper and glue it on the inside back of the card, centered in the window.

card inside

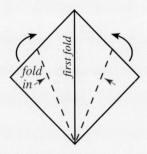

THE KITE FOLD: To form a kite shape, make the first fold diagonally. Unfold and turn the square on point. Fold in the left corner to the center fold. Repeat with the right corner. Turn the shape over to place.

- 5"x6½" Paper Flair™ white blank card
- Paper Flair™ Blossoms & Buds Paper Pack
- Paper Flair™ White, Cream & Laser Lace Petite Prints™ Paper Pack
- Paper Flair™ Painted Vellum Card Embellishments

1 Cut a 4½"x6" rectangle from the yellow roses paper; glue it centered on the card front.

2 Cut out two scallops from the laser lace, trimming off the bottom border on each. Position the straight edges together to form an oval and glue them centered to the card front.

3 Cut out the watering can vellum embellishment; mat it on yellow roses paper, leaving a ¹⁄₁₆" border. Glue the vellum embellishment to the center of the lace oval.

by Amy Gustafson

by Amy Gustafson

- 5"x6½" Paper Flair™ white blank card
- Paper Flair™ Burgundy & Rose Paper Pack
- Paper Flair™ White, Cream & Laser Lace Petite Prints™ Paper Pack
- Paper Flair™ Laser Words Card Embellishments
- X-acto® knife, cutting surface

1 Cover the card front with burgundy suede paper. Cut out a 4"x5½" rectangle from the pink stitches paper and glue it centered on the card front.

2 Cut the "Friends" laser embellishment, ¹⁄₁₆" from the outer edge of the motif. Glue it on a 2¾"x3½" burgundy suede rectangle. Place the matted motif on a cutting surface and use an X-acto® knife to cut out the letters in "Friends". Glue it centered on the card front.

3 Cut out two scallops from the laser lace, then cut each scallop in half. Glue one to each corner and trim the excess paper.

Lattice Cuts

Lattice cuts are wonderful additions to cards—especially with our luscious floral papers. We've used a few of our favorites, along with some special touches for you to create lovely cards. Although lattice looks complicated, it's rather easy to create. Just follow the simple cutting diagrams and instructions and you'll be amazed at how fast you can make your own lattice in minutes. Have fun!

by Susan Cobb

- *two 5"x6½" Paper Flair™ white blank cards*
- *patterned papers in this book*
- *(optional) Paper Flair™ Windows #1 Template*
- *(optional) Paper Flair™ Diamond Folds Template*
- *solid papers: yellow, black*
- *black pen (Zig® Writer)*
- *X-acto® knife, cutting surface*
- *tracing paper, transfer paper*

card inside

lattice pattern

1 Cut off ¾" from the opening edges of each card (both layers of both cards). With both cards open, overlap the left back of one card and the right back of the other card by 3½"; glue together.

2 Trace the lattice pattern on the right onto tracing paper; lay the pattern ½" from the top edge of the card, centered on the left fold; transfer the pattern then repeat the process on the right fold of the card. With an X-acto® knife, cut along the lines. Gently lift the first "V" and fold it upward. Repeat with every other "V".

3 Fold the right flap inward. Cut a 3⅝"x6½" rectangle of yellow paper; glue to the right flap, even along the open edges.

4 Fold the left flap inward. Cut a 3¾"x6¼" rectangle of yellow/black checks paper; mat it on black and cut a ⅛" border. Then glue it to the left flap.

5 Cut a 2¾" square from yellow and glue it centered ¾" below the top edge of the left flap. Trace a 2" window centered on the yellow square from the template. With the left flap open on a cutting surface, use the X-acto® knife to cut out the window.

6 Cut out the sunflower motif; glue it to the right flap, centered through the window. Outline the yellow inner window edge with the black pen.

- *5"x6½" Paper Flair™ white blank card*
- *Paper Flair™ Blossoms & Buds Paper Pack*
- *Paper Flair™ Painted Vellum Card Embellishments*
- *solid papers: dark purple, white, lavender*
- *silver pen (Zebra Jimnie Gel Rollerball)*
- *X-acto® knife, cutting surface*
- *tracing paper, transfer paper*

1 Cut 1" from the open edge of the card front. Cut a 3⅝"x6¼" rectangle from the purple pansies paper; glue it centered on the card front. Cut out the dragonfly vellum motif and mat it on lavender, leaving ⅛" border; then mat it again on white, leaving ¼" border. Glue it centered to the card front.

2 Cut out two 2"x6¼" rectangles of lavender; glue the backs together. Transfer the lattice pattern on page 76 onto the right long side of the lavender.

by Susan Cobb

3 Cut along each line to make 14 diagonal strips; trim off the lower right corner from the bottom strip and about ¾" along the top edge just above the inner mark of the first strip. Fold the first strip down so its tip is even with the opposing fourth strip, as shown in the diagram. Repeat the process with every other strip. Glue each folded strip in place.

fold strip

4 Outline the strips with the silver pen. Place the lattice piece on the edge of the inside front so it overlaps the dark purple inside back. Glue in place. Cover the inside back and inside front with purple paper.

card inside

- *5"x6½" Paper Flair™ white blank card*
- *Paper Flair™ Blossoms & Buds Paper Pack*
- *Paper Flair™ Pastel Vellum Paper Pack*
- *Paper Flair™ Painted Vellum Card Embellishments*
- *solid black paper*
- *9" of ⅜" wide lavender sheer ribbon with satin edges (Offray®)*
- *X-acto® knife, cutting surface*
- *foam adhesive tape*

1 Cover the card front with lavender vellum. Cut a 6"x4½" rectangle of black. Beginning at the upper left corner, cut fifteen 1" diagonal strips using the pattern on page 78. Fold down the first strip so its tip is even with the opposing fourth strip, as shown in the diagram above. Repeat the process with each alternating strip. Glue the rectangle centered on the card front.

by Susan Cobb

2 Cut a 4⅞"x4¼" rectangle of purple hydrangeas and glue it to the black rectangle as shown. Cut a 2½" black square, mat it on lavender vellum, leaving a 1/16" border and glue it centered on the hydrangea rectangle. Cut out the lavender vellum butterfly and attach it to the black mat with tiny pieces of foam tape just behind the body. Use the ribbon to make a shoestring bow and glue it to the upper left corner of the hydrangeas.

Mini Envelopes

Mini envelopes make opening a card twice as much fun. We've designed the perfect template for creating a perfect mini envelope—every time! It's called 2 Envelopes Template (see inside the back cover). Then, we put it to use with lovely patterned papers and vellums, as you can see below and on the next page. You may even want to include something special in your mini-envelopes—a small photo or memento will make these cards extra special.

by Lisa Garcia-Bergstedt

- 5"x6½" Paper Flair™ white blank card
- Paper Flair™ Burgundy & Rose Paper Pack
- Paper Flair™ Pastel Vellum Paper Pack
- solid white paper
- optional: Paper Flair™ 2 Envelopes Template
- black pen (Sakura® Gelly Roll™)
- 8" of ⅛" wide pink satin ribbon (Offray®)
- ⅜", ⅝", ⅞" wide heart punches (Marvy® Uchida)
- X-acto® knife, cutting surface
- tracing paper, transfer paper

1 Cover the card front with burgundy lace stripes. Cut a 5"x6⁷⁄₁₆" rectangle of burgundy moiré. Draw a 2¼"x1¹⁄₁₆" rectangle onto the moiré, angled slightly left near the top. Place on a cutting surface and use the X-acto® knife to cut out the window. Mat it on white, leaving a ¹⁄₁₆" border and cut the window to make a ¹⁄₁₆" white frame. Glue the moiré to the card front, angled to the left; trim off the excess corners.

2 Cover the inside back with burgundy hollow dots. Use the mini envelope template to trace the pattern onto the burgundy roses paper. Cut it out; fold the envelope sides toward the center. Mat the envelope bottom on white, leaving a ¹⁄₁₆" border. Fold in the bottom of the envelope and glue to secure. Trace around the envelope with the top unfolded onto pink vellum; cut out the shape and insert into the envelope. Glue the envelope to the inside back as shown, so it's centered in the window.

3 trace the envelope bottom only onto burgundy roses paper. Mat it on white, leaving a ¹⁄₁₆" border around the curve and ½" extension on the straight edge. Insert the extension between the card front and burgundy moiré, then glue in place.

4 Use the heart punches to make a variety of hearts from pink vellum, burgundy lace stripes and burgundy suede papers. Glue them randomly on a 5"x1¾" rectangle of white; trim along the top edge. Glue it to the inside bottom. Glue some additional hearts between the envelope and hearts border. Mat a burgundy lace heart on pink vellum and glue it to the window envelope bottom as shown. Use the ribbon to make a shoestring bow and glue it above the window. Write your messages on white, mat them on pink vellum and glue as shown.

card inside

mini envelope pattern

- *5"x6½" Paper Flair™ white blank card*
- *Paper Flair™ Purple Petite Prints™ Paper Pack*
- *solid white paper*
- *Paper Flair™ 2 Envelopes Template*
- *white pen (Marvy® Uchida)*
- *¾" wide heart punch (Marvy® Uchida)*
- *X-acto® knife, cutting surface*

1 Cut a 4⅞"x6¼" rectangle from the purple/lavender stripe paper; glue it centered on the card front. Cut a 2⅝"x3⅛" rectangle from the purple swirls paper; mat on white, leaving a 1/16" border. Glue centered on the card front ⅞" from the top edge.

2 Use the template to trace the mini envelope pattern onto the purple/lavender stripe paper; cut it out and fold in the sides. Mat the top and bottom flaps on white, leaving 1/16" border; fold in the flaps and mat the envelope on white, leaving a 1/16" border. Glue it centered on the matted swirl rectangle.

3 Use the punch to make a heart from the purple swirls paper; mat it on white, leaving a 1/16" border. Glue it to the envelope flap. With the white pen, write "sending you love" centered on the lower half of the card front.

by Amy Gustafson

by Amy Gustafson

card inside

- *5"x6½" Paper Flair™ white blank card*
- *Paper Flair™ Jewel Patterns Paper Pack*
- *Paper Flair™ Vellum Paper Pack*
- *Paper Flair™ Windows #2 Template*
- *Paper Flair™ 2 Envelopes Template*
- *white pen (Pentel Milky Gel Roller)*
- *X-acto® knife, cutting surface*

1 Open the card inside up on a cutting surface. Use the dull edge of the X-acto® knife to vertically score the center front and center back; fold the sides toward the center. Cover both front panels with the black with paisley and dots paper. Center the large heart template on the front of the card, about 1⅜" from the top of the card and trace it lightly in pencil.

2 Open the card and and place it face up on a cutting surface. Cut out each heart half from each panel. Close the card. Cut two ¼"x5" strips from the pink roses paper with a row of roses centered on the strip. Glue the strips along the top and bottom of the front panels about ⅛" from the edges. Trace along the edges of the strips and heart window with the white pen.

3 Cover the inside back of the card with the pink roses paper. Trace the small envelope on the dotted vellum, cut out, and fold. Trace around the edges of the envelope with the white pen. Center the envelope in the heart window and attach to the inside back of card.

4 Cut a 1⅛"x1⅝" rectangle from the pink roses paper. Mat it on the paisley paper, leaving a ⅛" border. With the white pen, outline the rectangle and write "I love you!" Tuck it in the envelope.

Mosaic

Mosaic cards can have regularly spaced, evenly cut elements (like the fireplace), or can be a random collection (like the rose). The choice is yours!

- 5"x6½" Paper Flair™ white blank card
- Paper Flair™ Burgundy & Gold Christmas Paper Pack
- Paper Flair™ Christmas Gold & Silver Vellum Card Embellishments
- solid white paper
- gold pen (Sakura® Gelly Roll™)
- X-acto® knife, cutting surface
- clear adhesive tape

1 Cover the card front with gold paper. Draw a 2⅝"x3¼" rectangle on the card front, centered 1" above the bottom edge. Open the card face up on a cutting surface and use the X-acto® knife to cut out the window.

2 Beginning at the bottom edge of the burgundy with gold dots paper, use a ruler to draw a line across the sheet every ⅜" (about 8-10 rows); cut out the strips. Cut the strips into ⅞" long "bricks". Beginning ⅛" from the top left corner, glue four bricks ⅛" apart; cut the fifth brick length to form a ⅛" gold border around the front edges. Start the next row ⅛" below with four bricks offset from the top row; cut one brick to fit at each end of the row. Repeat this process with 11 more rows to cover the card front.

by Amy Gustafson

3 Cut out two ⅛"x3½" and two ⅛"x2⅞" gold strips; glue them around the window as a frame. Cut out the fireplace motif centered in a 2¾"x3⅜" rectangle; use tape to attach it to the inside card front, centered in the window.

4 Open the card and cover the inside back with burgundy/gold mesh. With the gold pen, write "May the joys of the season warm your heart and fill your home!" on a 2½"x1½" rectangle of white; mat it on gold, leaving a ⅛" border. Glue it to the inside back, centered 1" below the top edge.

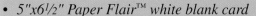

card inside

- 5"x6½" Paper Flair™ white blank card
- Paper Flair™ Jewel Patterns Paper Pack
- Paper Flair™ Pink Petite Prints™ Paper Pack
- Paper Flair™ Embossed Motifs Card Embellishments
- solid white paper
- X-acto® knife, cutting surface
- foam adhesive tape

1 Cut 1"x8½" strips from the dark pink dots, pink roses on black, and paisleys papers. Cut each strip into random shapes. Place the pieces on the card front, fitting them together as a mosaic, and leaving a 1/16" white border between the pieces and around the edge of the card. (Tip: To save time, don't fill in the part of the card front that will be covered by the rose motif.)

2 Cut the embossed rose motif into a 1¾"x4½" rectangle; mat it on the pink roses on black paper, leaving a 3/16" border. Mat it again on white, leaving a 1/16" border. Use foam tape to attach it to the card front, centered on the left side.

by Amy Gustafson

- *5"x6½" Paper Flair™ white blank card*
- *Paper Flair™ Purple & Blue Paper Pack*
- *Paper Flair™ Painted Vellum Card Embellishments*
- *black pen (Sakura® Gelly Roll™)*
- *foam adhesive tape*

1 Cover the card front with the purple moiré paper. Cut a 4¾"x6⅛" rectangle from the blue suede paper and glue it centered on the card front.

2 Cut forty ½" squares from the purple/blue dot paper and forty ½" squares from the purple sponged paper. Arrange them on the center of the card front in eight rows, leaving a 1/16" between them and a ¼" border around the outside.

3 Cut the dragonfly motif into quarters. Mat on purple *by Amy Gustafson* sponged paper, trimming evenly along the edges of the vellum. Mat them again as one piece on blue suede, leaving ⅛" between the pieces and around the outside. Mat again on lavender moiré, leaving a ⅛" border. Outline the edges of the card and the dragonfly square with black pen. Use foam tape to attach the dragonfly square to the center of the card front.

card inside

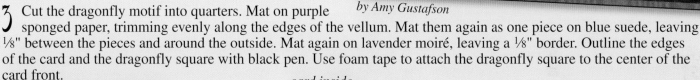

by Shauna Berglund-Immel

- *5"x6½" Paper Flair™ white blank card*
- *Paper Flair™ Purple & Blue Paper Pack*
- *Paper Flair™ Pastel Vellum Paper Pack*
- *Paper Flair™ Gold Patterns Paper Pack*
- *solid white paper*
- *5" of metallic gold thread*
- *white pen (Pentel Milky Gel Roller)*
- *¼" tall oval punch (Fiskars®)*
- *X-acto® knife, cutting surface*
- *tracing paper, transfer paper*

1 Trim 1¾" off the right side of the card front. Cover the front with purple moiré. Trace and transfer the window frame pattern onto the card front, ½" below the top edge. Open the card face up on a cutting surface and cut out the windows. Set two of the cut squares aside for step 4. Outline the windows with the white pen.

2 Cut a 2½"x3½" rectangle of clear vellum. Glue the vellum behind the windows. Cut a 1¾"x1⅝" rectangle of purple moiré; mat it on white, leaving a 1/16" border. Glue it centered on a 2"x2¼" rectangle of purple moiré; mat on white, leaving a 1/16" border. Glue it centered below the window frame. Use the punch to cut three ovals from gold. Cut a 1"x3/16" strip of gold. Glue an oval at each end of the strip to form a handle and the remaining to form a keyhole on the door as shown. Cut a strip of ⅛"x1¼" gold paper and glue between the windowpanes and door panel.

3 Cut 7/16" wide strips from the lavender mesh, lavender swirls, lavender/purple checks, purple dots, lavender dots and stars papers; cut some into squares and others into rectangles. Glue them in a mosaic pattern on the inside back to the right of the card front door. Cut a 3"x6¼" rectangle of lavender/purple diamonds and glue to the inside back, behind the door. Mat the two purple moiré squares from step 2 on white, leaving 1/16" borders. Glue to the inside back centered in the windows, with a 2½" length of thread looped above each. Use the white pen to write "Hi!" and "How are You?" on the squares.

Nested Shapes

Nested motifs are an exciting new way to create beautiful designs. It's like looking through a kaleidoscope of wonderful colors and patterns. The secret is stacking different patterns onto each other from large to small. Mixing and matching make it even more fun, with a host of possibilities to explore. Here are three cards to show how exquisite these motifs are in any format! So, get your template ready and start stacking these stunning shapes onto your cards.

by Susan Cobb

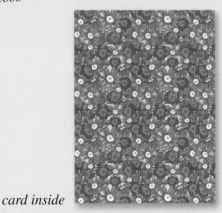

card inside

- 5"x6½" Paper Flair™ ivory blank card
- Paper Flair™ Teal Petite Prints™ Paper Pack
- solid pale yellow paper
- Paper Flair™ Nested Shapes Template
- white pen (Pentel Milky Gel Roller)
- foam adhesive tape

1 Cover the card front with dark teal stripes. Measure 4" from the top edge of card front and mark it on the right side edge. Place a ruler on the card front, diagonally between this point and the top left corner on the fold side; use a pencil to draw a line between the points. Cut along the line.

2 Trace the card front onto the pale yellow paper, adding ¹⁄₁₆" along the diagonal cut. Cut out the shape and glue it to the inside front.

3 Use the nested shapes template to make the following: pattern 2-A from the light teal dots, pattern 3-B from the dark teal dots, pattern 1-D from the light teal stripes and pattern 3-D from the dark teal dots. Cut each out; then mat each on pale yellow, leaving a ¹⁄₁₆" border.

4 Use foam tape to stack each of the two smallest motifs onto the dark teal dots motif; then glue the stack centered on the light teal dots motif. Glue the nested stack on the card front, with half extending beyond the upper edge.

5 Cover the inside back with the teal floral paper. Cut out a flower shape from the remaining floral paper; mat it on pale yellow, leaving a ¹⁄₁₆" border. Use foam tape to attach it centered on the nested stack. With the white pen, write your message as shown.

- *5"x6½" Paper Flair™ white blank card*
- *Paper Flair™ Teal Petite Prints™ Paper Pack*
- *Paper Flair™ Silver Patterns Paper Pack*
- *Paper Flair™ Nested Shapes Template*
- *optional: Paper Flair™ Windows #1 Template*
- *silver pen (Sakura® Gelly Roll™)*
- *foam adhesive tape*
- *X-acto® knife, cutting surface*

card inside

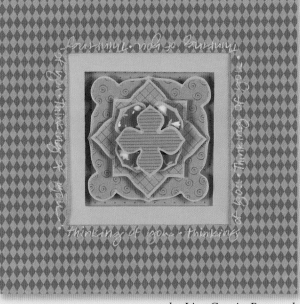

by Lisa Garcia-Bergstedt

1 Cut the card to 5" square. Cover the card front with teal diamonds. Open the card and place it face up on a cutting surface. Use the windows template and X-acto® knife to cut a 2¾" square from the center of the card front.

2 Cut a 3¼" square of silver. Place it on the cutting surface. Use the windows template to cut a 2⅛" square window from the silver square center. Glue the silver window frame to the inside front, centered in the card front window. Open the card and cover the inside back with light teal dots.

3 Use the nested shapes template to make the following: pattern 3-D from the teal stripes, pattern 2-D from the floral paper, pattern 1-D from teal mesh and pattern 1-C from the light teal swirls. Cut each out, then mat on silver, leaving a ¹⁄₁₆" border.

4 Use foam tape to stack from the largest to the smallest, rotating the designs as shown. Use foam tape to attach the nesting stack centered on the inside back, so it shows through the card front window. Use the silver pen to write "get well soon" above the nesting stack on the inside back and "Thinking of You" as a border around the card front window.

by Lisa Garcia-Bergstedt

card inside

- *5"x6½" Paper Flair™ white blank card*
- *Paper Flair™ Blue Petite Prints™ Paper Pack*
- *solid white paper*
- *Paper Flair™ Nested Shapes Template*
- *optional: Paper Flair™ Windows #1 Template*
- *foam adhesive tape*
- *X-acto® knife, cutting surface*

1 Place the card with the fold at the top. Cut a 6½"x2" rectangle of light blue dots and glue it to the card front, even with the lower edge. Use the windows template to draw four 1" squares centered along the blue dots rectangle. Open the card and place it on a cutting surface. Use the X-acto® knife to cut out the windows.

2 Cut a 3⅜"x6½" rectangle of blue flowers; mat it on white, leaving a ⅛" border only on one long edge. Glue it to the card front, with the matted edge even with the fold.

3 Cover the inside back with blue mesh paper. Print out or write "Happy Mother's Day!" on white paper; mat it on star paper, leaving a ¼" border. Mat it again on white paper, leaving a ⅛" border. Glue it centered on the inside back.

4 Use the nested shapes template to draw four 2-D patterns and four 3-D patterns on a variety of patterned papers. Mat each on white, leaving a ¹⁄₁₆" border. Use foam tape to stack a 2-D pattern onto a 3-D pattern. Use foam tape to attach each nesting stack to the inside back, so they are centered in each window. Cut out four dark blue flower shapes and attach them on top of each nesting stack with foam tape.

45

Paper Piecing

It's like applique, but with paper! Simply draw a design (like the party hats below) and cut them out of different papers. With paper piecing, you can make any card fit the theme you need!

by LeNae Gerig

- 5"x6½" Paper Flair™ white blank card
- Paper Flair™ Purple & Blue Paper Pack
- black pen (Zig® Millennium)
- ¼", ½" wide circle punches (McGill)
- ½" wide star punch (Marvy® Uchida)
- X-acto® knife, cutting surface
- tracing paper, transfer paper

1 Cut the card to 5" square. Cover the front with blue suede paper. Cut a 4⅜" square from the purple dotted paper and glue it centered on the suede.

2 Trace and transfer one hat pattern onto checked and another onto diamonds paper; transfer the hat rim pattern onto the blue dots on purple and the hat trim onto purple dots on blue. Cut them out and glue the hat trim to the bottom edge of the diamonds hat, then glue the rim piece on top. Use the punches to make circles and one star from the blue suede and glue them to the hats as shown. Use scissors to cut the fringe along the bottom of the diamonds hat and on its top.

3 Use foam tape to attach the hats to the card front as shown. Use the black pen to write "It's a Party" and streamers as shown on the card front.

- 5"x6½" Paper Flair™ white blank card
- patterned papers in this book
- solid papers: black, white
- black pen (Sakura® 3mm Micron)
- X-acto® knife, cutting surface

1 Open the card inside up on a cutting surface. Use the dull edge of the X-acto® knife to vertically score the center front and center back; fold the sides to meet at the center. Cover both front panels with black paper. Open the card and cover both inside panels and the inside back with black paper.

2 Cut out the patterned papers for this card in this book. Glue the purple plaid shirt pieces to the front panels as shown. Mat the tie pieces, collar and pocket each on black, leaving a 1/16" border. Glue the tie piece to the right side panel; extending beyond the edge. Glue the pocket on the right panel, even with the side fold. Glue the tie's knot and collar as shown.

3 Glue the t-shirt centered on the inside back. Use the pen to draw stitch marks around the t-shirt collar and sleeves, then around the shirt collar and pocket on the card front.

card inside

by Lisa Garcia-Bergstedt

46

- 5"x6½" Paper Flair™ white blank card
- Paper Flair™ Purple & Blue Paper Pack
- Paper Flair™ Pastel Vellum Paper Pack
- solid white paper
- black pen (Sakura® 3mm Micron)
- optional: fish die cut (Accu/Cut® Systems)
- X-acto® knife, cutting surface
- tracing paper, transfer paper

card inside

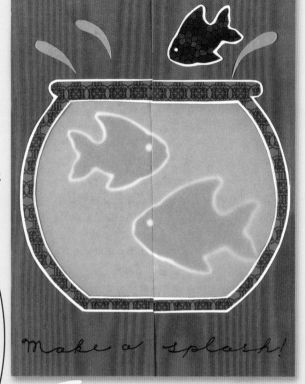

1 Open the card inside up on a cutting surface. Use the dull edge of the X-acto® knife to vertically score the center front and center back; fold the sides toward the center. Cover both front panels with purple moiré. Open the card and cover the inside back with purple swirls.

2 Trace and transfer the fish bowl pattern onto the right panel; flip it over and transfer the other half onto the left panel. Cut out each bowl half. Place white vellum over the bowl pattern and use a pencil to draw it ¼" larger on all sides. Cut it out and repeat for another vellum half. Trace and transfer the bowl outside onto the mosaic paper; then flip it over and repeat. Mat each mosaic piece on white, leaving a ⅟₁₆" border. Glue the matching vellum half to the mosaic back; then glue the half to the card front panel, so the straight sides are even along the center.

3 Trace and transfer each fish onto purple tile; mat each on white, leaving a ⅟₁₆" border. Glue the small fish to the right front panel as shown. Trace three splash patterns onto white vellum and glue them to the front as shown. Glue the remaining two fish to the inside back as shown above. Use the pen to write "Congratulations on your new endeavor!!" on the inside back and "Make a splash!" on the bottom of the card front panels.

by Lisa Garcia-Bergstedt

splash pattern

fish bowl

bowl outside

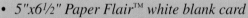

- 5"x6½" Paper Flair™ white blank card
- Paper Flair™ White, Cream & Laser Lace Petite Prints™ Paper Pack
- solid ivory paper
- black pen (Sakura® 3mm Micron)
- X-acto® knife, cutting surface
- foam adhesive tape
- tracing paper, transfer paper

1 Open the card inside up on a cutting surface. Use the dull edge of the X-acto® knife to score 4" from the left edge and 1" from the right edge; fold the sides toward the center. Cover both front panels with ivory/tan swirled paper. Open the card and cover the inside back with solid ivory. Cut a 1⅛"x6½" rectangle of ivory and glue it to the back of the 1" panel, so it extends ⅛" beyond the panel edge.

2 Turn the card with the narrow panel at the top. Trace and transfer the bow pattern onto the ivory/tan tiles paper. Use the X-acto® knife to cut out the center portions; then mat on ivory, leaving a ⅟₁₆" border.

3 Cut a 1¾"x10½" rectangle of hollow dots paper; mat on ivory, leaving a ⅟₁₆" border. Wrap it around the card as shown, with one end even with the bottom edge of the card and glue it over the folded end of the strip only. (The strip should slide on and off the card with ease.) Use foam tape to attach the bow to the strip. Use the pen to draw the bow outlines as shown.

by Lisa Garcia-Bergstedt

Paper Quilting

Quilting with paper is like quilting with fabric—working with coordinating patterns to create something entirely new, BUT without sewing! Bet you'll love it!

by Amy Gustafson

- 5"x6½" Paper Flair™ white blank card
- Paper Flair™ White, Cream & Laser Lace Petite Prints™ Paper Pack
- Paper Flair™ Laser Words Card Embellishments
- tracing paper, transfer paper

1 Cover the card front with the lace netting paper. Trace and transfer the 3½" circle pattern on page 78 onto the tan flecks and the ivory/tan swirled papers. Cut the tan flecks circle in quarters; cut the swirled circle into 16 slices using the pattern. Glue four swirled slices evenly spaced on each quarter circle of the tan flecks as shown.

2 Trace and transfer the lace quarter circle and cut four from the laser lace paper; carefully cut out each center design. Glue the centers to the inner corner of each fan; glue each fan to the remaining quarters of lace, leaving a ³⁄₁₆" lace border. Glue a fan to each corner of the card front as shown.

3 Cut out the laser embellishment "Thank You!" Mat it on tan flecks paper, leaving a ¹⁄₁₆" border. Glue it centered on the card front.

- 5"x6½" Paper Flair™ white blank card
- Paper Flair™ Purple & Blue Paper Pack
- Paper Flair™ Laser Words Card Embellishments

1 Cut a 4½"x6" rectangle from the purple sponged paper; glue it centered on the card front.

2 Cut out the following: four 1⅛" squares from purple dots on blue; two ¾" squares, two ¾"x3" and two 1½"x¾" rectangles from blue dots on purple; four 1½" squares from lavender/blue checked and one 1½"x3" rectangle of lavender stars on blue.

3 Glue one checked square to each corner on the sponged paper rectangle. Glue one of the longer blue dots on purple rectangles between the right top and bottom checked squares, with the right edges even. Repeat for the left side. Glue a smaller blue dots on purple rectangle between the two top checked squares, with the bottom edges even. Repeat for the bottom squares. Glue the stars rectangle centered inside the dotted rectangles.

4 Cut the two blue dots on purple squares diagonally and glue a triangle at each corner of the frame. Turn each purple dots on blue square on point and glue one to each corner as shown. Cut out the laser motif and glue it centered on the card front as shown.

by Amy Gustafson

- *5"x6½" Paper Flair™ ivory blank card*
- *Paper Flair™ Purple Petite Prints™ Paper Pack*
- *8" of ¼" ivory satin ribbon (Offray®)*
- *mini glue dots (Glue Dots, Inc.)*

1 Cut the card to 5" square. Cover the card front with lavender stripes. Cut a 4¾" square from the lavender mosaic paper and glue it centered on the card front.

2 Cut out the following: eight 1" squares and four ¾" squares from the purple roses, then eight 1" squares from the purple dots. Cut four 2³⁄₁₆" squares from lavender stripes.

3 Create a quilting block on each 2³⁄₁₆" square, with a floral square at the top left and lower right and a dots square at the top right and lower left, leaving a ¹⁄₁₆" border around the outer edges. Glue them to the front as shown, ⅛" apart. Mat each ¾" floral square on stripes, leaving a ¹⁄₁₆" border. Turn each on point and glue one centered on each quilt block.

4 Cut the ribbon into four 2" lengths. Tie a single knot in the center of each, then glue one centered on each floral diamond.

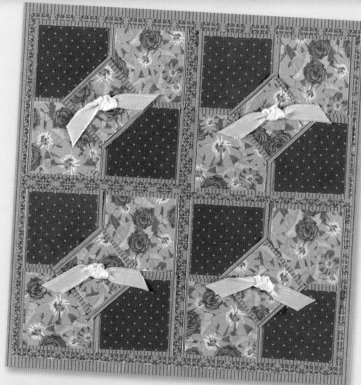

by Amy Gustafson

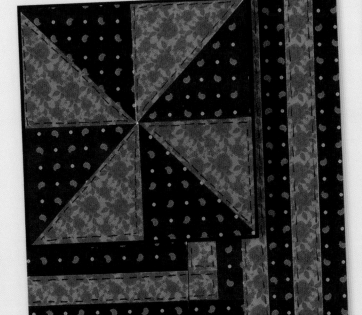

by Lisa Garcia-Bergstedt

- *5"x6½" Paper Flair™ white blank card*
- *Paper Flair™ Jewel Patterns Paper Pack*
- *solid black paper*
- *black pen (Sakura® 3mm Micron)*

1 Open the card inside up on a cutting surface. Use the dull edge of the X-acto® knife to vertically score the center front and center back; fold the sides toward the center.

2 Cut two 1¾" squares from the burgundy roses and two from the paisleys. Cut each in half diagonally to form triangles. Cut a 3⅝" square of black. Glue the triangles on the black square as shown. Glue the black square to the card front left panel, even with the top left corner. Open the card and cover the inside front panels and the inside back with black paper.

3 Cut ⅜" wide strips from the burgundy roses and from the paisleys. Glue three roses strips and four paisley strips to the card front left panel as shown, trimming them even with the card edges. Glue a 6½" long paisley strip along the fold on the right panel and a 2¹⁄₁₆" length along the bottom edge to form a backwards "L". Repeat with the roses strips, then again with paisleys, piecing each in place; repeat to cover the right panel. Use the pen to draw stitch marks along the edges of each burgundy roses piece.

Pin Pricking

This technique is an import from Holland, thanks to our Dutch card-maker, Leane. Who would have thought pricking paper with a pin would bring such wonderful results!

by Leane de Graaf

- 5"x6½" Paper Flair™ white blank card
- pricking pattern, patterned & solid papers in this book
- solid white paper
- large hat pin or sewing needle
- cutting surface

1 Cover the card front with solid red paper. Cut a 4¾"x6⁵⁄₁₆" rectangle of white paper and glue it centered on the card front. Cut a 4⅛"x5¾" rectangle of stitched navy and glue it centered on the card front.

2 Cut out the balloon pricking pattern (found in this book with the papers for this card). Cut out a red rectangle that is at least 4"x5½". Glue the pricking pattern to the back of the red paper rectangle.

3 Place the piece pattern side up on a cutting surface. Use the pin to prick the pattern. Cut around the outer edge, leaving a ⅛" border. Glue it centered on the card front.

4 Cut out the "Happy Birthday" message; mat it on white, leaving a ¹⁄₁₆" border. Glue it to the card front as shown.

- 5"x6½" Paper Flair™ ivory blank card
- pricking pattern, patterned & solid papers in this book
- large hat pin or sewing needle
- cutting surface

1 Cut a 4⅝"x6⅛" rectangle of teal floral paper and glue it centered on the card front.

2 Cut out the ivy pricking pattern (found in this book with the papers for this card). Cut out an ivory rectangle that is at least 4"x6". Glue the pricking pattern to the back of the ivory rectangle.

3 Place the piece pattern side up on a cutting surface. Use the pin to prick the pattern. Cut around the outer edge, leaving a ⅛" border. Glue it centered on the card front.

4 Cut out the "Best Wishes" message and mat on the teal stripes leaving a ¹⁄₁₆" border. Glue to the card front in the lower left as shown.

by Leane de Graaf

- 5"x6½" Paper Flair™ white blank card
- Paper Flair™ Blossoms & Buds Paper Pack
- Paper Flair™ Purple & Blue Paper Pack
- Paper Pizazz™ Vellum Cut-Outs™
- solid yellow paper
- pricking pattern (in this book)
- large hat pin or sewing needle
- cutting surface

1 Cover the card front with yellow. Cut a $4^{13}/_{16}$"x$6^5/_{16}$" rectangle of purple mesh paper and glue to the center of the card front.

2 Cut a 4"x5½" rectangle from the pansies paper; mat it on yellow, leaving a $^1/_{16}$" border. Glue it centered on the card front.

3 Cut out the pricking pattern (found in this book near the center of the patterned paper section). Cut out a 3½"x4" rectangle of yellow. Glue the pricking pattern to the back of the rectangle.

4 Place the piece pattern side up on a cutting surface. Use the pin to prick the pattern. Cut around the outer edge, leaving a $^1/_8$" border. Glue it centered on the card front. Cut out the vellum butterfly image and glue it on the pricked pattern as shown.

by Leane de Graaf

by Leane de Graaf

- 5"x6½" Paper Flair™ white blank card
- Paper Flair™ Blossoms & Buds Paper Pack
- Paper Flair™ Gold Patterns Paper Pack
- solid yellow paper
- rose pricking pattern (in this book)
- black pen (Sakura® Gelly Roll™)
- large hat pin or sewing needle
- cutting surface

1 Cover the card front with yellow paper. Cut a $4^5/_8$"x$6^3/_{16}$" rectangle of yellow roses paper; mat on gold, leaving a $^1/_8$" border. Glue it centered on the card front.

2 Cut out the rose pricking pattern (found in this book near the center of the patterned paper section). Cut out a 4" square of yellow paper. Glue the pricking pattern to the back of the square.

3 Place the piece pattern side up on a cutting surface. Use the pin to prick the pattern. Cut around the outer edge, leaving a $^1/_8$" border. Mat it on gold, leaving a $^1/_8$" border. Glue it centered on the card front.

4 Cut out a 3"x$^5/_8$" rectangle of yellow. With the black pen, write "Especially for You". Mat the rectangle on gold, leaving a $^1/_{16}$" border. Glue it centered below the rose motif as shown.

51

by Shauna Berglund-Immel

- *two 5"x6½" Paper Flair™ white blank cards*
- *patterned papers in the book*
- *9" of ⅝" wide lavender satin ribbon (Offray)*
- *white pen (Pentel Milky Gel Roller)*
- *black pen (Sakura® Gelly Roll™)*
- *X-acto® knife, cutting surface*
- *foam adhesive tape*

1 Cut one card to 5" square and the second card to 4⅞" square. Cut out the papers and embellishments for this card. Cover the first (larger) card inside front and back with the blue dotted paper. Cover the first card front with lavender stripes. Open the card face up on a cutting surface and use the X-acto® knife to cut out the circle, just inside the white outline.

2 On the smaller card, cover the front and inside front with the lavender flowers on green paper. Turn this with the fold at the bottom and open it. Open the first card and place the inside back on top of the upper half of the second card, so the window is on the left; then glue the two cards together.

3 Cut the support strips into two 2" and a 4" length. Fold one 2" the 4" strips lengthwise twice, with each fold ⁵⁄₁₆" deep, keeping the strips 2" and 4" long. With the purple leaf section face up, fold up the bottom ¾"; then glue the 4" support strip across its center back and the 2" strip near the top. With the blue dots section standing and the floral section flat, place the bottom of the purple leaves fold flat, facing forward, ⁵⁄₁₆" from the blue dots. Glue the support strips to the blue dots.

4 Glue the bottom tab of the floral bush to the folded tab of the purple leaves, so the bush stands upward. Glue the fence piece behind the bush, then fold the 2" support strip crosswise into thirds as shown by the diagram below. Glue one flap to the fence and the other to the leaves section.

5 Use foam tape to attach the butterflies to the card as shown. Glue the "take time..." piece to the opened floral section; then close the lower flap and glue the "Spring has Sprung!" piece to the green floral, so it is centered in the window. Use the ribbon to make a bow; glue it above the window as shown.

first panel

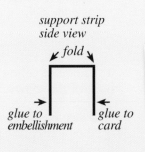

support strip side view

fold

glue to embellishment

glue to card

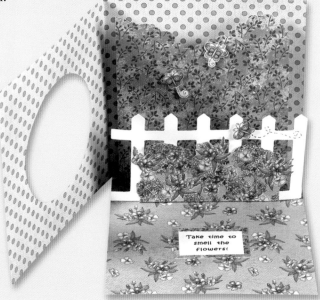

card inside

- 5"x6½" Paper Flair™ white blank card
- patterned papers in this book
- white pen (Marvy® Uchida)
- X-acto® knife, cutting surface

1 Cut the card to 5" square. Cut out the patterned paper pieces for this card. Glue the striped heart square on the card front and the hollow dots heart square on the inside front.

2 Place the card opened inside up on a cutting surface; cut only along the solid lines on the heart pattern, making certain not to cut on the dashed lines.

3 Cover the inside back with pink; then cut a 4⅞" square from the pink stripes and glue it centered on the inside back. Open the card and apply glue to the center heart only. Close the card and press the small heart into place to secure to the inside back. Outline the inside heart on the front with the white pen.

4 Cut out the "Sending you love" tag and glue it centered across the heart on the card front as shown. Cut out the "across the miles!" tag; glue it across the smallest heart, directly behind the front tag.

by Amy Gustafson

card inside

- 5"x6½" Paper Flair™ white blank card
- Paper Flair™ Silver Patterns Paper Pack
- black pen (Sakura® 3mm Micron)
- ⅞" wide heart punch (Marvy® Uchida)
- tracing paper, transfer paper

3-D present pattern

1 Cut the card to 5" square. Cut a 4⅝" square from the silver roses on pink paper. Glue it centered on the card front. Cut a 9¾"x4¾" rectangle of silver. Glue it centered on the card inside.

2 Trace and transfer the 3-D present pattern onto the back of the silver dots on pink paper. Cut out and fold it along the dashed lines; glue the top edge to the side to secure. Cut ¼" wide strips of silver: glue one on each side of the present, from the center bottom to the top point; then glue two 2" tails at the top point, trimming each end into a "V". Fold back the ends of a ¼"x1¾" length and glue; then wrap a ½" length around the center to form a bow. Glue it to the left side of the present top point.

3 Close the card and slide the present inside to make sure it lies flat properly. Use your finger to hold one side of the present to the card inside and glue the inside fold of the present to the card. Repeat for the other present side.

4 Trace and transfer the banner pattern (see page 77) twice onto silver. Cut out and mat one banner on silver pink roses, leaving a 1/16" border. Use the pen to write, "Happy Birthday!", then fold along the dashed lines and fold in half. Glue the banner tails to the card inside, above the present as shown. Write "Mom" on the remaining silver banner, then fold it along the dashed lines and glue it centered on the card front. Punch a silver heart and glue it above the front banner.

by Lisa Garcia-Bergstedt

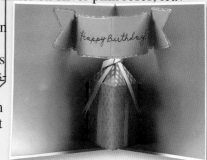

card inside

Pressed Flowers
You can use real pressed flowers or paper flowers that look pressed!

by Amy Gustafson

1 Cut a 4⅞"x6⅜" rectangle from the green dots paper; glue it centered on the card front. Cut out a 4¼"x5¾" rectangle from the green mesh paper; glue it centered to the card front.

- *5"x6½" Paper Flair™ white blank card*
- *patterned papers in this book*
- *1/16" wide hole punch (Family Treasures)*
- *16" of twine*
- *foam adhesive tape*
- *tracing paper, transfer paper*

2 Cut out the green dot pocket and fold the edges under along the dashed lines. Punch holes along the pocket sides, ⅛" from the edges and 3/16" apart. Cut a 10" length of twine. Thread one end of the twine through the pocket top left corner from the back to the front, then weave it in and out through the holes to resemble stitch marks; glue the twine ends to the pocket back. Attach the pocket to the card front with foam tape along the sides, positioning the pocket bottom ¾" above the lower card edge.

3 Punch two holes in each corner of the green mesh rectangle. Cut the remaining twine into four 1½" lengths; thread a piece through each pair of holes and tie the ends into a single knot at the front. Cut out the pressed flowers and leaves; insert them into the pocket and adhere in place, using foam tape on the flower and leaf in front.

- *5"x6½" Paper Flair™ white blank card*
- *Paper Flair™ Teal Petite Prints™ Paper Pack*
- *solid white paper*
- *black pen (Sakura® 3mm Micron)*
- *pressed yellow flower*
- *1¼" wide flower punch (Marvy® Uchida)*
- *tracing paper, transfer paper*

card inside

1 Trim 2½" off the right edge of the card front. Cut a 2⅜"x6½" rectangle of teal swirls and glue it to the front cover, even with the fold.

2 Open the card and cover the inside back with teal floral paper. Cut a 3" square from the teal diamonds; mat it on white, leaving a ⅛" border. Glue it centered on inside back. Use the punch to make a white flower. With the black pen, write "Thank You" on the flower and glue it centered on the teal diamonds.

3 Trace and transfer the flower pattern onto the light teal dots; cut it out and mat the left half of the flower shape on white, leaving a ⅛" border. Glue the matted half of the flower centered on the card front, with the unmatted side extending beyond the right edge. Glue the pressed flower to the teal flower center.

by Lisa Garcia-Bergstedt

- *5"x6½" Paper Flair™ ivory blank card*
- *Paper Flair™ White, Cream & Laser Lace Petite Prints™ Paper Pack*
- *Paper Flair™ Pastel Vellum Paper Pack*
- *6 pressed flowers*
- *Paper Flair™ Windows #1 Template*
- *48" of gold metallic thread, sewing needle*
- *gold pen (Pentel Hybrid Gelly Roll)*
- *X-acto® knife, cutting surface*
- *clear adhesive tape*

card inside

1 Cover the card front with tan flecks paper. Use the template to draw six 1½" squares on the card front, with the columns ½" apart and the rows ¼" apart. Open the card face up on a cutting surface and use the X-acto® knife to cut out each window. Use the gold pen to outline each window.

2 Cut a 5"x6½" rectangle of ivory netting paper. Position it on the inside back without gluing. Cut out the flower embellishments. With the card closed, position a flower centered in each window as shown and glue them to the inside back.

3 Cut six 1¾" tan vellum squares. Place a vellum square over a flower, so it is centered in a window. Holding the square in place, thread the needle with a single strand of gold thead and hand-stitch the square to the ivory netting paper. Secure the thread ends to the back of the paper with a small piece of tape. Repeat the process for the remaining five vellum squares; then glue the lace netting rectangle to the inside back of the card.

by Shauna Berglund-Immel

by Lisa Garcia-Bergstedt

- *5"x6½" Paper Flair™ white blank card*
- *Paper Flair™ Pink Petite Prints™ Paper Pack*
- *Paper Flair™ Pastel Vellum Paper Pack*
- *solid white paper*
- *white pressed flower with leaves*
- *20" of ¼" wide pink satin ribbon (Offray)*
- *X-acto® knife, cutting surface*

1 Cut a 4¾"x6¼" rectangle from the light pink dots paper and glue it centered on the card front.

2 Carefully tear a 3"x4" rectangle from the pink tile paper; mat it on white, leaving a ⅛" border. Tear two 1½"x2" rectangles each of white and pink vellums. Place them overlapping each other slightly and in alternating colors to form a 2¼"x3¼" rectangle centered on the pink tile mat and glue them in place. Glue the pressed flower centered on top of the squares.

3 Cut a 4¼" x5⅝" rectangle of white vellum. Place it centered on the card front and glue it at the four corners only. Cut the ribbon into four 5" lengths. Make a shoestring bow with each length and glue one to each corner on the white vellum.

Shaped Cards

Cards don't have to be square or rectangular. See the following three cards cut into shapes and one where the front flap is shaped. Lots of possibilities!

- 5"x6½" Paper Flair™ ivory blank card
- patterned papers in this book
- brown pen (Zig® Writer)
- 3" of ¹⁄₁₆" wide ivory satin ribbon (Offray®)
- ⅛" wide hole punch (McGill)
- X-acto® knife, cutting surface

1 Cut out the cup and glue it to the fold on the card front as shown. Open the card and cover the inside back with the ivory/tan swirl. Place the closed card on a cutting surface and use the X-acto® knife to cut out the shape. Open the card face up on the cutting surface and cut off the upper white area on the card front only. Cut out the saucer and glue it to the saucer shape on the card front.

2 Cut out the teabag tag and punch a hole in it. Slip one end of the ribbon into the tag hole and tie a knot to secure. Glue the tag to the card front as shown, with the ribbon extending up to the cup rim; trim off any excess ribbon. Use the pen to outline the inside and outside of the cup and saucer.

by Amy Gustafson

card inside

- 5"x6½" Paper Flair™ white blank card
- patterned papers in this book
- solid white paper
- white pen (Pentel Milky Gel Roller)

1 Cut out the purple dots on blue hat. Place the top along the fold on the card front as shown and glue it in place. Open the card and cover the inside back with the purple moiré. With the card closed, cut out the shape.

2 Cut out the hat trim, leaving a ¹⁄₁₆" white border along the top and bottom edges. Glue it to the card front as shown. Cut out the "Howdy Partner!" rectangle, leaving a ⅛" white border. Glue it centered on the hat trim. Cut out the "Happy Birthday Cowboy!" rectangle, leaving a ¹⁄₁₆" white border. Glue it centered on the checked star; then cut out the star, leaving a ¹⁄₁₆" white border. Glue the star centered on the inside back. Use the white pen to outline the card front and hat trim.

by Lisa Garcia-Bergstedt

card inside

- *5"x6¹/₂" Paper Flair™ white blank card*
- *Paper Flair™ Silver Patterns Paper Pack*
- *black pen (Sakura® Gelly Roll™)*
- *X-acto® knife, cutting surface*
- *tracing paper, transfer paper*

1 Trace and transfer the purse pattern (see page 79) onto the card front, with the handle on the fold. Place the closed card on a cutting surface and use an X-acto® knife to cut out the shape.

2 Trace and transfer the handle and buckle patterns onto silver and cut them out. Glue the handle to the card front. Transfer the purse pattern without the handle onto the silver leaves on blue paper; cut it out and glue it to the card front. Glue the buckle in place.

3 Use the black pen to outline the purse, handle and buckle and to draw stitches on the purse front as shown.

by Amy Gustafson

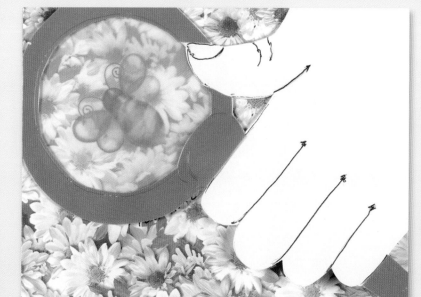

by Lisa Garcia-Bergstedt

card inside

- *5"x6¹/₂" Paper Flair™ ivory blank card*
- *Paper Flair™ Blossoms & Buds Paper Pack*
- *Paper Flair™ Pastel Vellum Paper Pack*
- *Paper Flair™ Gold Patterns Paper Pack*
- *Paper Flair™ Painted Vellum Card Embellishments*
- *black pen (Sakura® 5mm Micron)*
- *X-acto® knife, cutting surface*
- *tracing paper, transfer paper*

1 Trace and transfer the hand and magnifying glass pattern (see page 76) onto the card front, making sure to line it up on the fold as shown. Open the card face up on a cutting surface and use the X-acto® knife to cut out the shape. Use the black pen to draw the fingers and thumbnail on the hand.

2 Trace and transfer the two magnifying glass pieces onto gold; cut them out and glue to the card shape as shown. Trace the circular portion of the magnifying glass onto white vellum; cut it out, adding ¹/₄" extra around the outer edge and glue it to the back of the magnifying glass.

3 Open the card and cover the inside back with the white daisies paper. Cut out the bumble bee vellum motif and glue it to the upper left corner of the inside back so it is centered in the magnifying glass.

4 Use the black pen to write "I have discovered that you are a very special person. Hope you have a..." in a circle around the bee and "BEE UTIFUL DAY! HAPPY BIRTHDAY!!!" in a diagonal line between the circle and lower right corner as shown (under the handle).

Skeleton Leaves

Found in nature, skeleton leaves offer an interesting texture for cards. Now they're available in metallic colors which makes them even more fun to use.

by Amy Gustafson

- 5"x6½" Paper Flair™ white blank card
- Paper Flair™ Purple & Blue Paper Pack
- solid black paper
- one gold, one copper skeleton leaf (Black Ink)
- 2 yards of gold thread
- clear adhesive tape

1 Cover front of card with black paper. Cut a 4¾"x6¼" rectangle of lavender/blue oval tapestry paper. Tape one end of the thread to the tapestry back, wrap it across the rectangle in a random zig zag pattern, then tape the thread end to the back. Glue the rectangle centered on the card front.

2 Cut a 3"x4" rectangle from the blue suede paper; mat it on black paper, leaving a ⅛" border. Apply a small amount of glue to each end of the gold leaf and place it on the blue suede mat, angled to the upper right. Apply a small amount of glue to each end of the copper leaf and place it on top of the gold leaf, angled in the opposite direction.

- 5"x6½" Paper Flair™ ivory blank card
- Paper Flair™ White, Cream & Laser Lace Petite Prints™ Paper Pack
- Paper Flair™ Pastel Vellum Paper Pack
- gold pen (Pentel Hybrid Gel Roller)
- gift tag #3 die cut (Accu-cut® Systems) (pattern on page 77)
- three ⅜" wide ivory buttons
- 12" of metallic gold thread
- 12" of ¼" wide sheer tan ribbon (Offray®)
- 3 gold skeleton leaves (Black Ink)
- 3 gold eyelets (Stamp Studio)
- foam adhesive tape
- tracing paper, transfer paper

by Shauna Berglund-Immel

1 Cut a 6¼"x4¾" rectangle of tan flecks, a 6"x4½" rectangle of tan vellum and a 5¾"x4¼" rectangle of ivory netting. Use the gold pen to outline each rectangle. Glue the netting centered on the vellum, then the vellum centered on the flecks; glue the layered rectangle centered on the card front.

2 Trace and transfer the tag pattern (see page 77) to make three tags: one of tan swirls, one of ivory swirled and one of tan dots; repeat to make three tan vellum tags. Use the gold pen to outline each vellum tag. Layer a vellum tag over each patterned tag and fasten them together with an eyelet at the top as shown. Cut the ribbon into 4" lengths and knot one through each eyelet, trimming the ends diagonally.

3 Glue a skeleton leaf on each tag. Insert one end of the thread through a button, wrapping it through each hole and knotting it on top to secure. Repeat for the two remaining buttons. Glue one button to each tag as shown. Attach the tags evenly spaced on the card front with foam tape.

- 5"x6½" Paper Flair™ white blank card
- Paper Flair™ Purple & Blue Paper Pack
- solid black paper
- silver pen (Pentel Hybrid Gel Roller)
- 2 silver skeleton leaves (Black Ink)
- X-acto® knife, cutting surface
- tracing paper, transfer paper

1 Open the card and place it inside up on a cutting surface. Use the dull edge of the X-acto® knife to score a line 2½" from each side; fold each side in toward the center, forming flaps. Cover both flaps with black paper. Cut two 2⁷⁄₁₆"x6¼" rectangles of blue/purple diamonds and glue one to each front flap, with the center edges meeting and creating a ⅛" border on the top, bottom and outer sides.

2 Trace and transfer the larger red flap pattern (see page 78) onto black and the smaller blue pattern onto the blue stitches paper. Cut both out, then glue the small flap on the large. Fold ½" under on the longest edge and glue this portion to the top back edge of the card, with the pointed flap wrapping to the front.

3 Layer the leaves at slightly different angles and glue them to the flap point. With the silver pen, write "for you" on a 1" square of black; slip the lower left corner under one leaf and glue in place.

by Amy Gustafson

by Amy Gustafson

- 5"x6½" Paper Flair™ white blank card
- Paper Flair™ Blue Petite Prints™ Paper Pack
- Paper Flair™ Silver Patterns Paper Pack
- Paper Flair™ Embossed Motifs Card Embellishments
- silver skeleton leaf (Black Ink)
- foam adhesive tape

1 Cut the card to 5" square. Turn the card with the fold on top. Cover the card front with silver paper. Cut a 4¾" square from the light blue swirls paper. Glue it centered on the card front.

2 Cut three 1⅛"x4⅜" strips from the dark blue swirls paper. Mat each on silver, leaving a ¹⁄₁₆" border. Glue the strips evenly spaced on the card front as shown.

3 Glue the leaf to the card front angled from the upper left to the lower right corner. Tear around the edges of the embossed ladybug motif; mat it on silver, leaving a ⅛" border. Use foam tape to attach the ladybug square on the card front, angled as shown.

Stickers

Want to add a colorful embellishment to your card quickly and easily? Just add a sticker! Those used here are printed on clear material so no white edge shows. So easy!

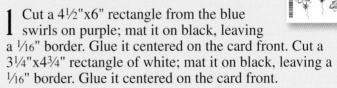

- *5"x6½" Paper Flair™ white blank card*
- *Paper Flair™ Purple & Blue Paper Pack*
- *Paper Pizazz™ Ruth Ninneman's Balloons Stickers*
- *solid papers: white, black*
- *black pen (Marvy® Uchida)*

1 Cut a 4½"x6" rectangle from the blue swirls on purple; mat it on black, leaving a ¹/₁₆" border. Glue it centered on the card front. Cut a 3¼"x4¾" rectangle of white; mat it on black, leaving a ¹/₁₆" border. Glue it centered on the card front.

2 Cut a 3" square from the blue/purple checks paper. Cut it in half diagonally to form two triangles. Take one triangle and fold the longest side over ¼", wrong sides together, to form a slightly smaller triangle. Trim off the overhanging corners, then mat the triangle on black, leaving a ¹/₁₆" border on the two shorter sides.

3 Glue the triangle on the card front as shown. Place the stickers above the triangle. With the black pen, write "Need a Lift?" above the stickers.

by Amy Gustafson

- *5"x6½" Paper Flair™ white blank card*
- *Paper Flair™ Soft Patterns Paper Pack*
- *solid papers: yellow, white*
- *Paper Pizazz™ Annie Lang's Baby #2 Stickers*
- *black pen (Marvy® Uchida)*
- *foam adhesive tape*

1 With the card fold at the top, trim 1¾" off the right side of the card front. Cut a 4¼"x4½" rectangle of the lavender dots on blue; mat it on yellow, leaving a ⅛" border. Glue it centered on the card front. With the stripes horizontal, cut a 6"x4½" rectangle of lavender stripes; mat it on yellow, leaving a ⅛" border. Glue it centered on the inside back. Use the black pen to outline each yellow rectangle.

2 Cut a 2½"x2¾" rectangle of purple stripes; mat on white, leaving a ¹/₁₆" border. Adhere a baby sticker in the center. Use foam tape to attach the rectangle to the center of the card front.

3 Cut three ¾" squares of white. Place a heart sticker centered on each. Attach them to the inside back, evenly spaced along the right side of the card as shown, using foam tape. Use the black pen to write "Congratulations on your new little love!" on a 2¼"x1⅜" rectangle of white; mat it on yellow, leaving a ¹/₁₆" border. Glue it on the inside back, centered within the area covered by the card front.

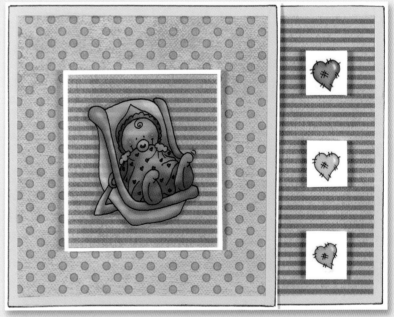

by Amy Gustafson

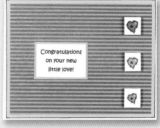

card inside

- *5"x6½" Paper Flair™ white blank card*
- *Paper Flair™ Pink Petite Prints™ Paper Pack*
- *Paper Pizazz™ Janie Dawson's Girlfriends Stickers*
- *solid white paper*
- *black pen (Sakura® Gelly Roll™)*
- *15" of white ⅞" wide satin ribbon (Offray®)*
- *foam adhesive tape*

1 Cut a 4⅞"x6⅜" rectangle of pink stripes paper and glue it centered on the card front. Glue a length of ribbon to the center of the card front as shown. Use the remaining ribbon to make a shoestring bow with 1" loops. Glue the bow on the ribbon 1½" above the bottom edge of the card front.

2 Place the friends sticker on white and cut, leaving a ¹⁄₁₆" white border. Mat it on pink dots; leaving a ⅜" border; mat again on white, leaving a ¹⁄₁₆" border. With the pen, outline the outer edge of the sticker, the pink dots rectangle and the pink stripes rectangle on the card front. Use foam tape to attach the sticker mat centered on the card front between the bow and top edge of the card.

by Amy Gustafson

- *two 5"x6½" Paper Flair™ white blank cards*
- *Paper Flair™ Soft Patterns Paper Pack*
- *solid yellow paper*
- *Paper Pizazz™ Janie Dawson's Busy Kids Stickers*
- *optional: Paper Flair™ Windows #1 Template*
- *green glitter pen (Sakura® Gelly Roll™)*
- *X-acto® knife, cutting surface*

1 Open the card flat. Use the dull edge of the X-acto® knife to vertically score the center front and center back; fold each side toward the center. Cover both front panels with white dots on green paper. Cut two ¼"x6½" strips of yellow and glue one along each opening edge of the front panels.

2 With the panels closed, use the template to draw a 1½" square centered between the panels; then use the template to draw a 1" square near the upper left corner, one 1¼" from the bottom edge on the left panel, one near the lower right corner and one even with top edge of the center square. Open the card face up on the cutting surface and use the X-acto® knife to cut out each square.

3 With the second card closed, trim ¹⁄₁₆" off the top and opening edges. Cover the inside back with the sunflowers paper. Open the card face up on the cutting surface and cut a ½" half circle into the card front, 2¼" from the bottom edge. Glue the back of the second card to the inside back of first card. Close the flaps and place the stickers centered in the windows as shown.

4 Write messages on white rectangles and mat each on yellow, leaving ⅛"-¼" borders. Glue them to the first panel and card inside as shown. Use the pen to draw a "— • —" border inside each window and loopy lines along the yellow borders on the front flaps.

card front with panels open

card inside

by Lisa Garcia-Bergstedt

Tea Bag Folding

Tea bag folding originated in Holland in the 1990's as a unique way to use the pretty packages covering tea bags. It has become a popular paper crafting technique with designs in beautiful patterned papers. It's a technique we can't resist in card making, and soon you'll become hooked, as well. It's easy for you to start. Just follow the folding diagrams below to make the simple diamonds we've used for the exquisite cards on this page and the next.

large triangle pattern

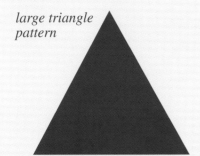

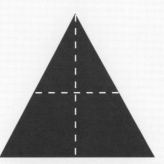

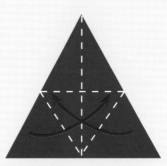

1 Trace and transfer the triangle shape to paper. Cut it out.

2 Fold it in half, then unfold. Fold in half horizontally, then unfold. Use the center crease to fold in each side to the center.

3 Fold the lower left corner to the right edge, then fold the lower right corner to the left edge.

4 Turn the diamond face up and place it in your design.

by LeNae Gerig

- 5"x6½" Paper Flair™ white blank card
- Paper Flair™ Blossoms & Buds Paper Pack
- Paper Flair™ Gold Patterns Paper Pack
- Paper Flair™ White, Cream & Laser Lace Petite Prints™ Paper Pack
- X-acto® knife, cutting surface
- tracing paper, transfer paper

1 Cover the card front with red roses paper. Trace and transfer the triangle pattern on page 78 onto the card front and cut out the shape.

2 Glue ivory netting paper to the inside back of the card. Cut the bottom edge from the laser lace border and glue it centered on a 6½"x1¼" strip of gold. Glue the gold strip ½" from the bottom edge of the ivory netting.

3 Use the small triangle pattern on page 63 to draw five triangles of gold and five triangles of laser lace. Cut them out; then follow the diagrams above to fold each into a diamond shape. Glue them centered on the card front in an alternating pattern to form a circular shape.

card inside

- *5"x6½" Paper Flair™ white blank card*
- *Paper Flair™ Burgundy & Rose Paper Pack*
- *tracing paper, transfer paper*

1 Trim 1¼" off the open edge of the card front. Cover the inside with burgundy herringbone paper. Cover the card front with burgundy suede. Cut a 3⅜"x6¼"burgundy roses paper and glue it centered on the burgundy suede.

2 Use the pattern on page 62 to cut six large triangles of burgundy tri-dots and the pattern below to cut six small triangles of burgundy herringbone. Cut them out; then follow the diagrams on page 62 to fold each triangle into a diamond shape. Glue the burgundy tri-dot diamonds into a star shape on burgundy suede, then cut out the star shape, leaving a ¹⁄₁₆" border. Mat each herringbone diamond on burgundy suede, leaving a ¹⁄₁₆" border and glue them to the dotted star as shown. Glue the star to the bottom front of the card with 1" extending beyond the lower edge as shown.

small triangle pattern

by LeNae Gerig

by LeNae Gerig

- *5"x6½" Paper Flair™ white blank card*
- *Paper Flair™ White, Cream & Laser Lace Petite Prints™ Paper Pack*
- *Paper Flair™ Embossed Motifs Card Embellishments*
- *optional: Paper Flair™ Windows #1 Template*
- *deckle patterned scissors (Family Treasures)*
- *foam adhesive tape*
- *tracing paper, transfer paper*

1 Cut a 4¾"x6¼" rectangle from the ivory flourishes paper; glue it centered on the card front.

2 Use the triangle pattern on page 62 to cut 12 large triangles of checked and the pattern above to cut 10 triangles of herringbone. Cut them out; then follow the diagrams on page 62 to fold each into a diamond shape. Glue one row of six checked diamonds ¼" from the card front top edge as shown. With foam tape, glue a row of five herringbone diamonds on top, each centered between two checked. Repeat along the bottom of the card front.

3 Cut four 1" squares from the ivory swirl paper. Use foam tape to attach them to the center of the card front, forming a 2" square. Cut out the embossed dragonfly motif with decorative scissors and glue it centered on the swirl squares.

Tent

Tent cards add a stately emphasis to your message that stands on its own. We've updated the look with gorgeous motifs, striking colors and moving parts—the result will make a lasting affect for your loved ones and friends. Tent cards are easy to make. Simply open your card face down and score 1" along each end as shown with the dashed lines in the diagram (use the dull edge of your X-acto® knife). Then, just cut ½" in on each end, fold in on the score lines and slip the cuts together for the tent. It's that easy!

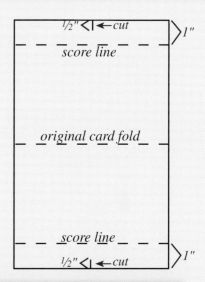

by Amy Gustafson

- 5"x6½" Paper Flair™ white blank card
- Paper Flair™ Purple & Blue Paper Pack
- Paper Flair™ Embossed Motifs Card Embellishments
- optional: Paper Flair™ Windows #1 Template
- solid white paper
- 8" length of silver metallic thread
- sewing needle
- X-acto® knife, cutting surface
- clear adhesive tape

1 Open the card face down on a cutting surface. Use the dull edge of the X-acto® knife to score a line 1" from each edge, as shown in the diagram above. Cut a ½" slit into the card centered on each scored flap, as shown. Draw a 2¾" square window ⅝" from the left edge, center fold and scored line; use the X-actor® knife to cut the window.

2 Cut a 6⁵⁄₁₆"x3⅞" rectangle of blue suede. Place the rectangle on a cutting surface and cut a 3" square on the left end, ⁷⁄₁₆" from the top, side and bottom edges. Glue the suede rectangle to the card, with the window centered on the card window. Cut a 2⅛"x2¾" rectangle of blue/purple diamonds. Mat it on white and cut, leaving a ⅛" border. Glue the rectangle to the card front, centered between the window and right edge.

3 Cut out the embossed butterfly motif. Cut the thread in half; thread the needle with a single strand and pierce one hole through the center bottom of the butterfly. Remove the needle and pull the thread ends even. Use tape to attach the thread ends to the inside card front below the window. Repeat the process to attach the upper portion of the butterfly to the inside front above the window.

4 Cut a 6½"x4" rectangle of white stitches on blue; glue it to the inside back, between the fold lines. Print or write "Thinking of You" on a 1"x1½" rectangle of white paper and glue it centered on the diamonds rectangle as shown. Fold the flaps under at the scored lines, then slide the slits together to form a tent.

card inside

- 5"x6½" Paper Flair™ white blank card
- Paper Flair™ Blue Petite Prints™ Paper Pack
- solid yellow paper
- gold pen (Pentel Hybrid® Gel Roller)
- 1⅛" long moon punch, ½" wide star punch (Family Treasures)
- 24" of gold metallic thread
- sewing needle
- X-acto® knife, cutting surface
- clear adhesive tape

by Amy Gustafson

1 Open the card face down on a cutting surface. Score lines as shown in the diagram on page 64. Cut a ½" slit as shown in the diagram. Cut a 4"x6½" rectangle from the blue stars paper; glue it to the inside back between the fold lines.

2 Cut a 4"x6½" rectangle of blue mesh; glue it on the card front, between the fold lines. Open the card face down on a cutting surface. Draw a 1¾"x5¼" rectangle centered on the card front ⅝" from the top fold. Use the X-acto® knife to cut it out to make a window.

3 Punch out one moon and six stars from yellow and outline each with the gold pen. Use the needle to insert the thread through the card fold in seven spots spaced apart. Tie to secure and trim so each spot has 1"-2" of a single thread extending to the inside. Tape a star to six and a moon to the seventh thread. Tie a shoestring bow with the thread and glue on the moon.

4 Outline the window and the card front with gold pen; write "Welcome, little one!" in gold centered below the window. Fold the two flaps under on the scored lines, then slide the slits together to form a tent.

- 5"x6½" Paper Flair™ white blank card
- Paper Flair™ Gold Patterns Paper Pack
- Paper Flair™ Embossed Motifs Card Embellishments
- solid black paper
- gold luster rub-on (Craf-T Products)
- gold pen (Pentel Hybrid Gel Roller)
- X-acto® knife, cutting surface

by Amy Gustafson

1 Open the card face down on a cutting surface. Follow the diagram and instructions on page 64 to score lines and cut slits. Cover the card front with a 6½"x4" rectangle of gold dots.

2 Cut a 5¾"x3⅛" rectangle of gold/black checks; mat it on black, leaving a 1/16" border. Cut a 5¼"x2⅞" rectangle of red/gold diagonal stripes; mat it on black, leaving a 1/16" border. Cut a 4¾"x2⅜" rectangle of gold; mat it on black, leaving a 1/16" border. Glue the layers together, then glue to the card as shown.

3 Cut out the embossed "Happy Birthday" motif with its border intact. Use your finger to brush the gold luster onto the embossed designs and border. Use the pen to outline the letters and inner frame. Mat the embossed motif on black, leaving a 1/16" border. Glue it centered on the gold rectangle. Fold the two flaps under on the scored lines, then slide the slits together to form a tent.

3-Dimensional

Cards don't have to be flat! A twig, wire, beads and more add a clever twist to any card. Let's see how....(also, see pages 74 & 75).

by Amy Gustafson

1 Cut the card into two pieces along the fold. Cover one piece with the green pinstripes paper; outline the edges with the brown pen.

- 5"x6½" Paper Flair™ white blank card
- patterned papers in this book
- brown pen (Zig® Writer)
- 5" length of twine
- 5" long twig
- ⅛" wide hole punch (Family Treasures)
- X-acto® knife, cutting surface

2 Trim the second piece to 5"x5½". Use the dull side of the X-acto® knife to score a line ½" from the narrow edge, and another line ¾" from the first scored line. Fold back the first scored line and glue it to the top back of the green pinstripes section, so the remaining portion wraps onto the front.

3 Cover the front with the green leaves paper. Cut a 5"x¾" rectangle from the green pinstripes paper and glue to the top edge of the card front. Outline the edges with the brown pen.

4 Use the punch to make a hole on each side of the top section. Cut the twine in half. Make a loop, wrap it around one end of the twig and pull the ends of the twine through the loop; then thread the twine through the front hole on the card and tie it in a knot at the back. Repeat for the other hole.

card inside

5 Cut out the verse and glue it centered on a 2"x1½" rectangle of green pinstripes, outlining each in brown. Cut out the individual leaves and glue them to the message frame as shown. Cut out the leaf border and glue it to the inside back as shown.

- 5"x6½" Paper Flair™ white blank card
- Paper Flair™ Silver Patterns Paper Pack
- Paper Flair™ Painted Vellum Card Embellishments
- rusted wire (Westrim Crafts)
- foam adhesive tape
- glue dots (Glue Dots Inc.)
- X-acto® knife, cutting surface
- transfer paper, tracing paper

1 Cut a 4¾"x6¼" rectangle of silver and glue it centered on the card front. Cut a 4⅛"x5⅝" rectangle of pink roses and glue it centered on the silver.

2 Trace and transfer the hat pattern (see page 76) onto the pink dotted paper. Cut it out and mat on silver, leaving a 1/16" border. Cut the hatband from silver and glue as shown. Cut out two vellum daisies. Glue one overlapping the other and use foam tape to atach them to the left side of the hat as shown.

3 Create the hat stand using the pattern as a guide for bending the wire. Adhere the hat stand to card front with glue dots. Use foam tape to adhere the hat at the top of the stand.

by Lisa Garcia-Bergstedt

- 5"x6½" Paper Flair™ ivory blank card
- Paper Flair™ Gold Patterns Paper Pack
- solid rust red paper
- gold pen (Sakura® Gelly Roll™)
- beads: 7 gold bugle, 4 red bugle, 24 gold seed, 40 red & orange seed (Art Accents)
- 10" of 24-gauge copper wire (Artistic Wire Ltd.)
- ⁵⁄₁₆" wide heart punch (Family Treasures)
- foam adhesive tape

by Lisa Garcia-Bergstedt

card inside

1 Trim 1" off the open edge of the card front. Cover the card front with the gold dot paper. Cut a ¾"x6½" strip each of gold and red papers. Glue the red strip to the inside front, with ¼" extending beyond the open edge of the card front. Glue the gold strip behind it, so it extends ⅛" beyond the red strip.

2 With the gold pen, write "A little bit of love..." on a 2½"x⅜" rectangle of red, mat it on the gold roses paper, then mat it on gold, leaving ⅛" borders both times.

3 Cut out a 3" square of gold and mat it on red, leaving a ¹⁄₁₆" border. Slide the beads in random order onto the wire, curling the wire ends. Bend the beaded wire into a 1¾" wide and 2" tall heart and glue it centered on the gold square. Use foam tape to adhere the square to the card front as shown. Glue the message so it tucks under the heart square as shown.

4 Open the card and cover the inside back with gold roses. Write "goes a long way!" in gold on a 3"x2" rectangle of red. Punch a heart in the upper left corner, then mat the rectangle on gold, leaving a ⅛" border. Glue the rectangle centered on the inside back.

by Susan Cobb

1 Cut a 4⅛"x5⅝" rectangle of teal dots and mat it on teal mesh, leaving a ³⁄₁₆" border. Glue it to the card front. Cut a 3⅝"x4⅝"

- 5"x6½" Paper Flair™ ivory blank card
- Paper Flair™ Teal Petite Prints™ Paper Pack
- Paper Flair™ Pastel Vellum Paper Pack
- white pen (Pentel Milky Gel Roller)
- 9" of ¹⁄₁₆" wide ivory satin ribbon (Wrights®)
- foam adhesive tape

rectangle of dark teal stripes and glue it centered on the card front. Cut a 3½"x4" rectangle of light teal stripes and glue it even with the right side teal mesh, 1¼" from the card bottom edge.

2 Cut a 4⁹⁄₁₆" long and three squares wide strip of teal mesh. Glue it centered on a 4⁹⁄₁₆"x1" strip of teal filegree. Glue it on the card front, even with the sides of the patterned papers and ½" above the bottom edge of the light teal stripes rectangle.

3 Cut a 2" square of teal vellum, using the diagram on page 79, fold it into a bouquet holder. Glue the center of the ribbon to the back of the bouquet holder so each side wraps to the front; tie it in a shoestring bow to secure. Glue the holder on the card front as shown.

4 Cut two 2" wide clusters of teal flowers and two single blossoms from the teal floral paper. Slip one cluster into the bouquet holder, angled left. Use foam tape to adhere the second cluster in the holder, angled right. Use foam tape to adhere one single blossom in the center of the second cluster and the other blossom at the upper left of the first cluster. Use the white pen to write "Thank You" in the upper left of the light teal stripes square.

3-D Score & Fold

Creating 3-dimensional looks in paper is easy with a few folds, tucks and foam tape. We've provided patterns, like this star, to get you started. Simply cut out the outer shape and fold along each line. There are a few points where a snip is necessary to create lift. Foam tape adds extra height, though the folds alone can give the pattern "height" as we've shown on page 69 with the vellum triangle. If you're unsure of folding with your pretty papers, practice with a piece of scrap paper first. It's easier than you think!

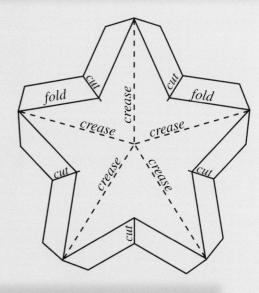

by Susan Cobb

- *5"x6½" Paper Flair™ white blank card*
- *Paper Flair™ Purple & Blue Paper Pack*
- *Paper Flair™ Vellum Paper Pack*
- *solid white paper*
- *white pen (Pentel Milky Gel Roller)*
- *10" of ⅞" wide lavender sheer ribbon*
- *foam adhesive tape*
- *transfer paper, tracing paper*
- *X-acto® knife, cutting surface*

1 Cover the card front with purple moiré. Cut a 4⅜"x5¾" rectangle of purple stars on blue and mat it on white, leaving a ¹⁄₁₆" border. Glue it center to the card front. Cut a 3¼" square of vellum lavender diamonds; glue it centered on the card front.

2 Draw a 2¾" window centered in the vellum square. Open card face up on a cutting surface and use the X-acto® knife to cut out the window. Cover the card inside with purple sponged paper.

3 Trace and transfer the star pattern onto the back of the purple moiré paper. Cut out the outer shape and along the five lines in the inner corners. With the patterned side face down, fold in the edges along each outer line; then make creases along the dashed lines using the dull edge of your X-acto® knife. Unfold so the outer crease appears on the patterned side of the star. Place a ½" square of foam tape in the star center back. Glue the star to the inside back so it is centered in the window. Use the ribbon to make a shoestring bow and glue it to the upper left corner as shown. Use the white pen to outline the window.

card inside

- *5"x6½" Paper Flair™ white blank card*
- *Paper Flair™ Silver Patterns Paper Pack*
- *solid papers: white, black*
- *30" of silver metallic thread*
- *silver skeleton leaf (Black Ink)*
- *foam adhesive tape*
- *transfer paper, tracing paper*
- *X-acto® knife, cutting surface*

1 Cover the card front with black paper. Cut a 4¾"x6¼" rectangle of pink dotted paper; glue it centered on the card front.

2 Trace and transfer the rectangle pattern (see page 78) onto the back of the pink roses paper. Cut out the outer shape. With the patterned side face down, fold in the edges along each outer line; then use the dull edge of your X-acto® knife to make creases along the dashed lines. Place foam tape on the back to fill the 2"x3" center of the rectangle. Mat the rectangle on black, leaving a ⅛" border. Glue it to the card front as shown.

3 Cut a 1¾"x2⅝" black rectangle and mat it on white, leaving a 1/16" border. Glue one end of the silver thread to the rectangle back; then wrap the thread randomly around the rectangle several times and glue the other end to the back to secure. Glue the skeleton leaf on the rectangle. Glue the leaf rectangle centered on the 3-D rectangle.

by Susan Cobb

by Shauna Berglund-Immel

- *5"x6½" Paper Flair™ white blank card*
- *Paper Flair™ Blossoms & Buds Paper Pack*
- *Paper Flair™ Pastel Vellum Paper Pack*
- *Paper Flair™ Silver Patterns Paper Pack*
- *transfer paper, tracing paper*
- *X-acto® knife, cutting surface*

1 Trim the card to 5" square. Cut one 4½" square each from blue vellum and the blue floral papers. Glue the vellum square on top of the floral square in the center only; mat it on silver, leaving a ⅛" border. Glue the matted square centered on the card front. Cut a 3¼" square from the blue floral paper and mat it on silver, leaving a ⅛" border. Glue it centered on the card front.

2 Place blue vellum over the triangle pattern (see page 76) and use a pencil to trace the purple and black lines. Cut out the outer shape. Use the dull edge of the X-acto® knife to score along the dashed lines only. Trace and transfer the triangle only (black line pattern) onto the back of the blue floral paper; cut out the floral triangle. Place the floral triangle face up behind the vellum, then fold the vellum tabs to the back of the floral triangle. Cut three blue flowers from the floral paper and glue to the triangle center; then glue the triangle to the card front as shown.

1 Trim a 5"x2¼" rectangle off the top of the card front. Cut out the patterned paper shapes from this book. Glue the quilted shape on the card front; then trim off the upper right corner along the edge of the quilt.

- 5"x6½" Paper Flair™ white blank card
- patterned papers in this book
- scallop decorative scissors (Fiskars®)
- 10 " of ⅛" wide pink satin ribbon (Offray)
- foam adhesive tape
- X-acto® knife, cutting surface

2 Cover the inside back with dark pink stripes. Cover the inside front with the light pink stripes rectangle, but don't trim it; close the card and wrap the top right corner onto the card front and glue to secure. Mat the pillow on white and trim with decorative scissors. Attach it to the top of the inside back with foam tape.

3 Glue the dark pink dots paper to the back of the light pink dots. Place it on the cutting surface and use the X-acto® knife to cut out the window along the white line on the dark pink side. Fold it in half to form a miniature card. Use a pencil to lightly mark

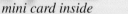

the inside window. Glue the single rose square to the marked square. Glue the message rectangle below. Glue the ribbon center to the mini card back, then glue the card to the main card front as shown. Wrap the ribbon around the mini card and tie it in a shoestring bow.

by Shauna Berglund-Immel

mini card inside   card inside

- 5"x6½" Paper Flair™ white blank card
- Paper Flair™ Burgundy & Rose Paper Pack
- solid white paper
- Paper Flair™ Embossed Motifs Card Embellishments
- pink glitter pen (Sakura® Gelly Roll™)
- small, large scallop decorative scissors (Fiskars®)
- X-acto® knife, cutting surface

1 Cut the card to 5" square. Cover the card front with burgundy moiré paper. Cut a 4½" square from the pink diamonds paper and mat it on white, leaving a 1/16" border. Glue it centered on the card front.

2 Cut out the embossed heart with bow and mat on burgundy moiré paper, leaving a ⅛" border. Cut a 2½"x4½" rectangle of white and fold it in half. Glue the embossed heart centered on the folded paper and cut to a heart shape, leaving the fold intact. With the pink pen, write "Happy Valentine's Day" on the inside back, then glue it centered on the card front.

card inside

by Amy Gustafson

- 5"x6½" Paper Flair™ white blank card
- Paper Flair™ Burgundy & Rose Paper Pack
- Paper Flair™ Painted Vellum Card Embellishments
- optional: Paper Flair™ Windows #1 Template
- black, pink pens (Sakura® Gelly Roll™)
- X-acto® knife, cutting surface

card inside

by Amy Gustafson

1 Use the template to draw a 2¼"x3" rectangle on the card front, 1¼" from the top edge and centered between the sides. Open the card face up on a cutting surface and use the X-acto® knife to cut out the window. Cut a 4¾"x6¼" rectangle of pink diamonds paper. Turn the rectangle over and use a pencil to mark 1" from the left and right edges and ¾" from the top, then use the marks to draw a 2¾"x3½" rectangle and cut it out. Glue the diamonds paper face up and centered on the card front.

2 Cut the vellum cake embellishment to 1¾"x2⅜". Cut a 1¾"x4¾" rectangle of white paper and fold it in half. Place the fold at the top and glue the vellum embellishment on it. With the black pen, write "Happy Birthday To You!" on the inside back and outline the front with the pink pen.

3 Cut 3"x4" rectangle from pink swirls and glue the back of the mini card centered in the rectangle, so it opens by lifting up the bottom edge. Place the rectangle on the inside back of the card so it is centered in the window and glue in place.

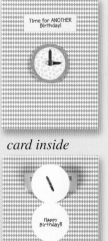

card inside

clock inside

by Lisa Garcia-Bergstedt

- two 5"x6½" Paper Flair™ ivory blank cards
- Paper Flair™ White, Cream & Laser Lace Petite Prints™ Paper Pack
- solid papers: ivory, dark brown
- Paper Flair™ Windows #2 Template
- black pen (Sakura® Gelly Roll™)
- ⅛" wide hole punch (McGill)
- one brass brad
- X-acto® knife, cutting surface

1 Cover the card front of one card with ivory swirls. Cut a 1"x6½" strip of herringbone and mat it on ivory, leaving a 1/16" border on the long sides. Glue it centered on the card front. Open the card face up on a cutting surface. Use the template and X-acto® knife to cut a 2¼" circle from the center of the card front.

2 Cover the inside back with the diamonds paper. Draw a 2" circle on the fold of the second card and cut it out to form a round mini card. Cover the front with the tan dots paper. Cut a 1½" circle from the tan swirls paper and mat on ivory, leaving a 1/16" border. Punch a hole in the circle center. Cut two hands for the clock (see pattern below) from brown paper and glue one at 12:00 and at 3:00. Insert the brad and bend the ends to flatten. Glue it centered on the mini card front.

3 Glue the back of the clock card on the diamonds, centered in the window. With the black pen, write "Happy Birthday!!". Write "Time for ANOTHER Birthday!" on a 2¾"x¾" rectangle of ivory and glue it above the clock.

clock hand pattern ➡

Vellum

It adds a wonderful look to cards. Whether the vellum is a pretty pastel color, diminuitive dots or lovely lace, you'll love the look you'll get!

by Amy Gustafson

- *5"x6½" Paper Flair™ white blank card*
- *Paper Flair™ Blossoms & Buds Paper Pack*
- *Paper Flair™ Vellum Paper Pack*
- *Paper Flair™ Gold Patterns Paper Pack*
- *optional: Paper Flair™ Windows #1 Template*
- *black pen (Sakura® Gelly Roll™)*
- *15" of ³⁄₈" wide sheer black ribbon with satin edges (Offray®)*
- *X-acto® knife, cutting surface*

1 Turn the card with the fold at the top. Cover the card front with gold paper. Cut a 4¾"x6¼" rectangle from the red roses paper, making sure a prominent rose is featured near the lower left corner. Glue it centered on the card front.

2 Cut a 4½"x6" rectangle of the tri-dot vellum. Using the 2" square template, cut a window in the lower left corner of the vellum to feature the prominent rose when centered on the card front; then glue in place.

3 Glue a length of ribbon across the card 1" below the fold. With the remaining ribbon, tie a shoestring bow with ½" long loops. Cut the tails at an angle and glue as shown. With a black pen, write "With Love" centered in the lower right corner of the card front.

- *5"x6½" Paper Flair™ white blank card*
- *Paper Flair™ Burgundy & Rose Paper Pack*
- *Paper Flair™ Pastel Vellum Paper Pack*
- *Paper Flair™ Vellum Paper Pack*
- *24" of ⅛" wide pink satin ribbon (Offray®)*
- *mini glue dots (Glue Dots. Inc.)*
- *X-acto® knife, cutting surface*

card inside

1 Cover the card front with pink diamonds. Draw a 3"x4½" rectangle centered on the card front. Open the card face up on a cutting surface and use the knife to cut the window from the front.

2 Cut a 5"x3½" vellum dots paper; then cut another, placing one sheet behind the other and lining up the dots.

3 Tear out hearts by hand, four from the light pink and five from dark pink vellums, varying the sizes. Place them in random order on one vellum dots rectangle; glue them in place, then glue the other vellum dots on top, making sure the dots are in line. Glue the vellum rectangle to the inside card front, centered in the window. Open the front, glue ribbon around the window to form a frame. Use the remaining ribbon to make a shoestring bow and glue it to the frame bottom. Tear three smaller hearts from dark pink vellum. Glue one to each upper corner of the window. Glue one heart in the lower right corner of the inside back.

by Lisa Garcia-Bergstedt

72

- 5"x6½" Paper Flair™ white blank card
- Paper Flair™ Burgundy & Rose Paper Pack
- Paper Flair™ Pastel Vellum Paper Pack
- solid white paper
- 9" of ⅝" wide pink sheer ribbon (Offray®)
- silver pen (Sakura® Gelly Roll™)
- foam adhesive tape

1 Cut the card to 5" square. Cover the card front with the stitches on pink paper. Cut a 4⅛" square of white and a 4½" square of dark pink vellum; glue the vellum centered on the white. With the vellum side on top, glue the square centered on the card front. Cut a 4" square of pink roses and glue it centered on the vellum square, so a ¹⁄₁₆" border from the white square (now light pink) frames the roses square.

2 Use the pattern to cut the two small hearts; cut one envelope from the dark pink vellum. Fold the envelope on the dashed lines, folding the bottom flap up last and glue in place. Glue the dark pink vellum heart on the top of the white heart.

3 Outline the small heart card and envelope edges with the silver pen. Write "Happy Valentine's Day!" on the small heart card. Glue the envelope and card overlapping as shown. Cut two individual roses from the pink roses paper and attach them to envelope and small heart card with foam tape. Use the ribbon to make a shoestring bow and glue to the bottom of the heart.

by Susan Cobb

envelope pattern

cut 1 white and 1 dark pink vellum heart

by Amy Gustafson

- 5"x6½" Paper Flair™ white blank card
- Paper Flair™ Burgundy & Rose Paper Pack
- Paper Flair™ Vellum Paper Pack
- black pen (Marvy® Medallion)
- 20" of ¼" wide rose satin ribbon (Offray)

1 Trim 3¼" from the card front, so it is 1¾" wide. Cover this flap with burgundy clover paper. Glue a length of ribbon along the flap center. Use the remaining ribbon to tie a shoestring bow with ½" long loops and glue as shown.

2 Cut a 5½"x6½" rectangle of pink diamonds paper. Align it on the inside back, folding the excess on the right side to the back of the card and glue only the folded edge to the back.

3 Cut a 3⅞"x6½" rectangle from the lace with dots vellum, positioning the lace along the left side. Glue the left edge of the vellum to the inside front of the front flap face up, with the right vellum edge even with the right edge of the card. Close the card. With the black pen, write "Thank You" on the bottom right corner of the vellum.

Wire

There are so many choices for wire—plastic-coated with bright colors, gold, copper or silver—just to name a few. We find mini glue dots are terrific for attaching wire to paper.

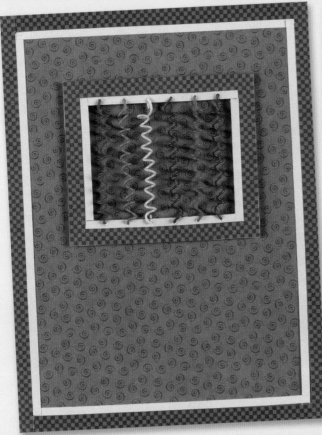

by Amy Gustafson

- *5"x6½" Paper Flair™ white blank card*
- *Paper Flair™ Purple & Blue Paper Pack*
- *solid papers: yellow, white*
- *5" lengths of plastic-coated wire: red, green, yellow, purple, orange, blue*
- *X-acto® knife, cutting surface*
- *foam adhesive tape*
- *cotton swab*

1 Glue purple/blue checks to cover the card front. Cut a 4¼"x5¾" of swirls. Mat it on yellow, leaving a ⅛" border. Glue it centered on the card front.

2 Cut a 3"x2½" rectangle from the purple/blue checks paper; glue it to white and trim the edges even. Cut out a 2¼"x1¾" rectangle window from the center of the checks. Cut two 2½"x⅛" strips and two 2"x⅛" strips of yellow; glue them along the inner edge of the window.

3 Poke six holes, evenly spaced, along the top and bottom of the yellow border in the window frame. Wrap each piece of wire around a cotton swab handle; feed the wire ends through two opposite holes to the back of the window frame and fold the ends down to secure. Repeat for all the wires. Attach the window frame centered 1" below the top edge of the card front with foam adhesive tape evenly distributed around the frame.

- *5"x6½" Paper Flair™ white blank card*
- *Paper Flair™ Jewel Patterns Paper Pack*
- *solid papers: black, white*
- *optional: pole, fish die cuts (Accu/Cut® Systems)*
- *12" of 24-gauge copper wire*
- *Victorian patterned scissors (Fiskars®)*
- *mini glue dots (Glue Dots, Inc.)*
- *X-acto® knife, cutting surface*

card inside

1 Trim ¼" from the right edge of the card front, then trim off 1⅛" from the bottom of the card front. Cover the inside back with the purple/green stripes paper, leaving the floral border along the bottom as shown. Cover the card front with the purple tile paper; trim the right edge with patterned scissors.

2 Use the patterns to cut the pole and two fish from black. Curl the left end of the copper wire into a swirl, place it on the reel of the pole, then bend the wire to form scallops connecting each loop and curl and cut the wire at the pole end. Glue the pole and wire to the front as shown. Pierce through a fish with another piece of wire, looping it at the end to secure, leaving 2½" wire length remaining. Attach the other end to the pole wire.

3 Write your message on a 3½"x⅝" rectangle of white paper and mat on black, leaving a ⅛" border. Glue it to the inside back with the remaining fish above it as shown.

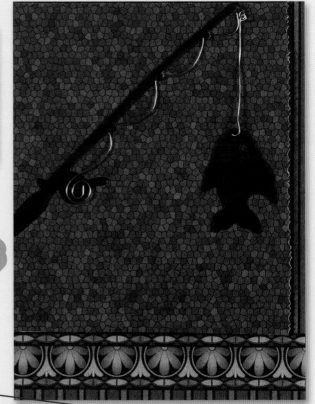

by Lisa Garcia-Bergstedt

74

- *5"x6½" Paper Flair™ white blank card*
- *Paper Flair™ Purple Petite Prints™ Paper Pack*
- *solid white paper*
- *four ⅜" wide silver sparkle clear acrylic star beads (The Beadery®)*
- *28" of 24-gauge silver wire*
- *mini glue dots (Glue Dots, Inc.)*

1 Cut a 4¾"x6¼" rectangle from the purple stars paper; glue it centered to the card front.

2 Cut the wire into four 7" lengths. Fold each length in half, then twist one section around the other. Thread a bead onto each wire.

3 Cut a 2¼"x4¼" rectangle from the purple swirls paper; mat it on white, leaving a ⅛" border. Insert the end of beaded wire into each side of the white mat ⅝" from one end, bending the ends to the back. Repeat with the three remaining beaded wires 1" apart. Slide the beads to alternating sides, then glue each in place. Glue the rectangle centered on the card front.

by Amy Gustafson

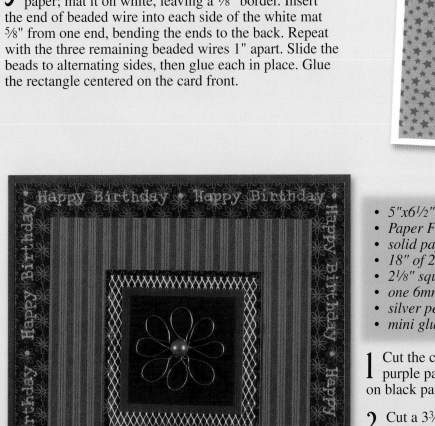

by Amy Gustafson

- *5"x6½" Paper Flair™ white or ivory blank card*
- *Paper Flair™ Jewel Patterns Paper Pack*
- *solid papers: purple, black*
- *18" of 24-gauge silver wire*
- *2⅛" square of silver wire mesh (WireForm®)*
- *one 6mm purple bead*
- *silver pen (Pentel Gel Roller)*
- *mini glue dots (Glue Dots, Inc.)*

1 Cut the card to 5" square. Cover the card front with purple paper. Cut a 4¾" square from the blue daisies on black paper and glue it centered on the card front.

2 Cut a 3¾" square of the purple/teal green stripe paper and glue it centered on the card front. With the silver pen, write "Happy Birthday" around the edge of the daisies square. Cut a 2¼" square of black with daisies paper and glue it centered on the card front. Cut a 2⅛" square of wire mesh and use glue dots to attach it to the center of the card front.

3 To form the daisy, first form one petal loop on one end of the wire and slide the bead onto it. Form another petal loop out of the other side of the bead, then wrap the wire around the base of each petal loop once (next to the bead) and form the other six petal loops by making three figure eights and keeping the intersections of the wire behind the bead.

4 Cut a 1½" square of black paper and mat it on purple, leaving a ⅛" border. Attach the wire daisy to the black square using a glue dot, then attach it to the center of the wire mesh.

Patterns

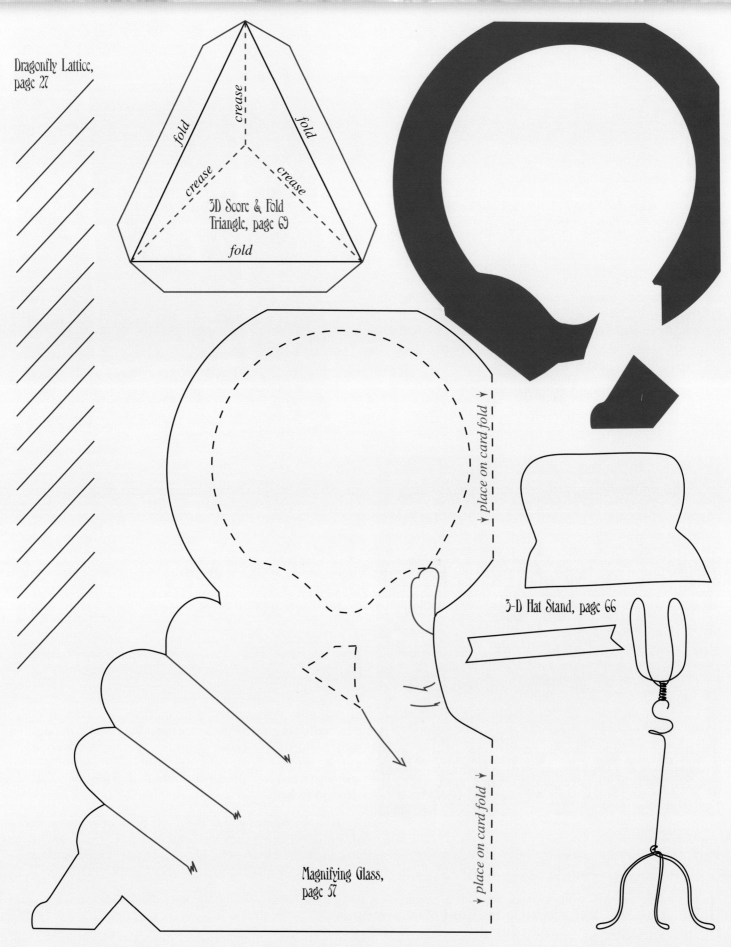

Dragonfly Lattice,
page 27

fold

crease

fold

crease

crease

3D Score & Fold
Triangle, page 69

fold

place on card fold

3-D Hat Stand, page 66

place on card fold

Magnifying Glass,
page 57

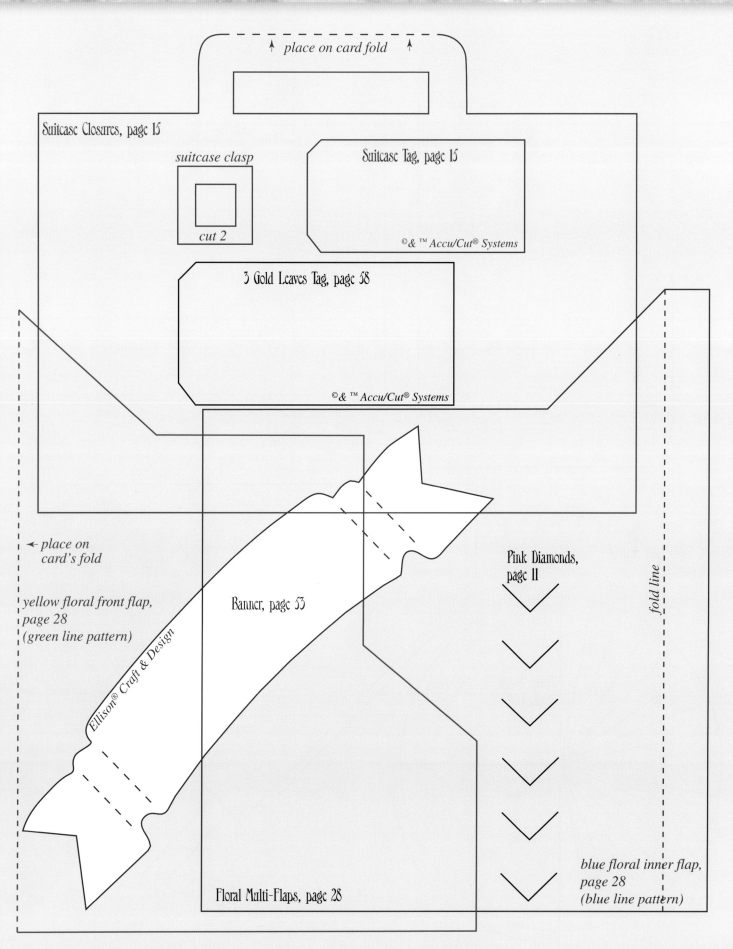

place on card fold

Suitcase Closures, page 15

suitcase clasp

cut 2

Suitcase Tag, page 15

©& ™ Accu/Cut® Systems

3 Gold Leaves Tag, page 58

©& ™ Accu/Cut® Systems

← place on
card's fold

yellow floral front flap,
page 28
(green line pattern)

Ellison® Craft & Design

Banner, page 53

Pink Diamonds,
page 11

fold line

blue floral inner flap,
page 28
(blue line pattern)

Floral Multi-Flaps, page 28

Patterns

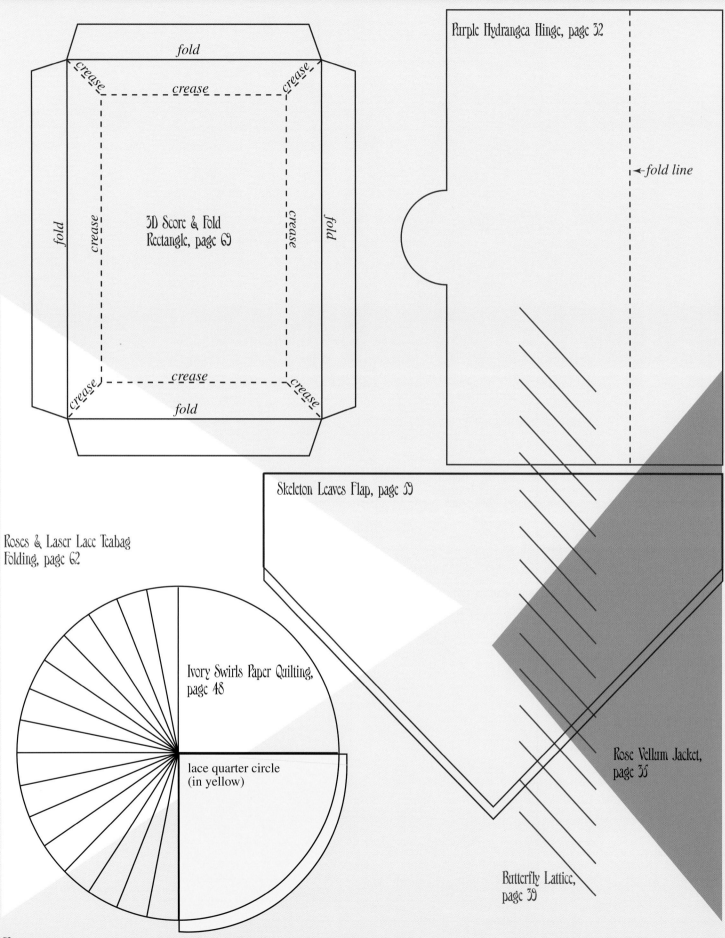

fold

crease

crease

crease

fold

crease

3D Score & Fold
Rectangle, page 69

crease

fold

crease

crease

crease

fold

Purple Hydrangea Hinge, page 32

←fold line

Skeleton Leaves Flap, page 59

Roses & Laser Lace Teabag
Folding, page 62

Ivory Swirls Paper Quilting,
page 48

lace quarter circle
(in yellow)

Rose Vellum Jacket,
page 36

Butterfly Lattice,
page 39

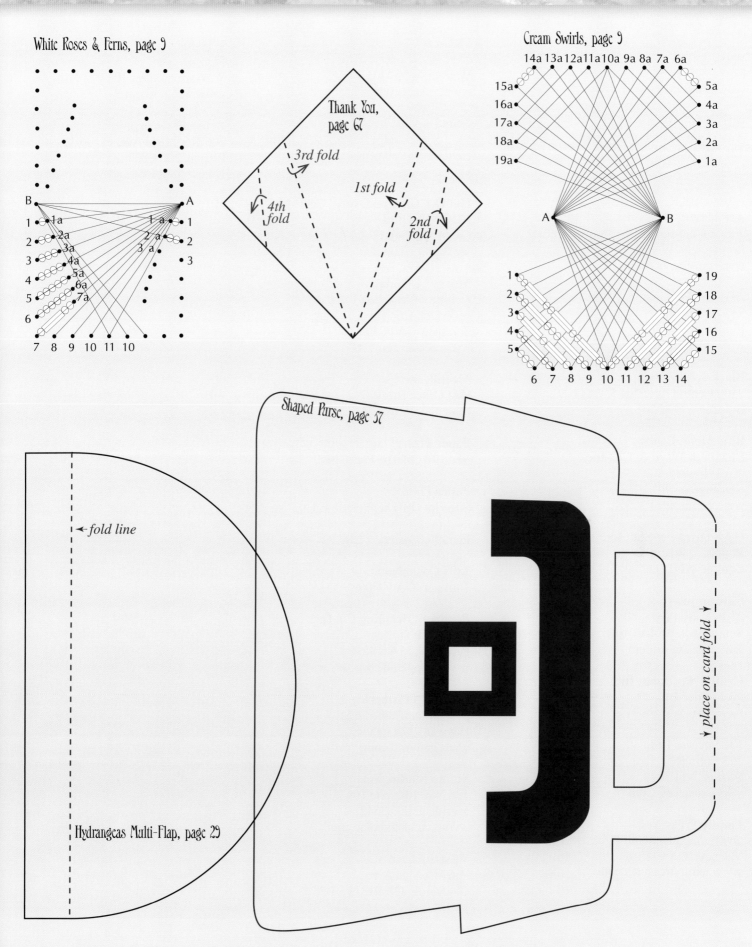

White Roses & Ferns, page 9

Cream Swirls, page 9

Thank You,
page 67

1st fold

2nd fold

3rd fold

4th fold

Shaped Purse, page 57

← fold line

place on card fold →

Hydrangeas Multi-Flap, page 29

Manufacturers & Suppliers

Accu/Cut Sytems
1035 E Dodge St.
Fremont, NE 68025
www.accucut.com

AMACO®
American Art Clay Co., Inc.
4717 W 16th St.
Indianapolis, IN 46222
www.amaco.com

Art Accents
205 E. Chestnut St.
Bellingham, WA 98225
www.artaccents.net

Artistic Wire
752 N. Larch Ave.
Elmhurst, IL 60126
www.artisticwire.com

Black Ink
2300 Central Ave., Ste K
Boulder, CO 80301

Blue Moon Beads
Elizabeth Ward & Co., Inc.
4218 Howard Ave.
Kensington, MD 20895
www.beads.net

C.M. Offray & Son, Inc.
Route 24, Box 601
Chester, NJ 07930

Canson Inc.
21 Industrial Dr.
South Hadley, MA 01075
www.canson-us.com

Craft-T-Products, Inc.
Post Office Box 83
Fairmont, MN 56031

EK Success Ltd.
125 Entin Rd.
Clifton, NJ 07014
www.eksuccess.com

Family Treasures
24922 Anza Dr., Unit D
Valencia, CA 91355
www.familytreasures.com

Fiskars®
7811 W. Stewart Avenue
Wausau, WI 54401
www.fiskars.com

Glue Dots Int'l
5575 S. Westridge
New Berlin, WI 53151
www.gluedots.com

Hot Off The Press, Inc.
1250 NW Third, Dept. B
Canby, OR 97013
www.paperflair.com

Marvy® Uchida
Uchida of America Corp.
3535 Del Amo Blvd.
Torrance, CA 90503
www.uchida.com

McGill, Inc.
Post Office Box 177
Marengo, IL 60512

Paper Pizazz™
(see Hot Off The Press, Inc.)

Paper Flair™
(see Hot Off The Press, Inc.)

Pentel of America Ltd.
(pens)
2805 Columbia St.
Torrance, CA 90509

Pepperell Braiding Co, Inc.
22 Lowell St.
Pepperell, MA 01463
www. pepperell.com

Sakura® of America
30780 San Clemente St.
Hayward, CA 94544
www.gellyroll.com

Stamp Studio, Inc,
124 NW 10th, Ste 101
Meridian, ID 83642
www.stampstudioinc.com

Westrim Crafts
9667 Canoga Ave.
Chatworth, CA 91311

Wrights
PO Box 398
W. Warren, MA 01092
www.wrights.com

Zebra Pen Corp.
105 Northfield Ave.
Edison, NJ 08837
www.zebrapen.com

CHALKING, page 10

Or write
your own
message
here

←

Friends are like
quilts...
they are a great
source of comfort!

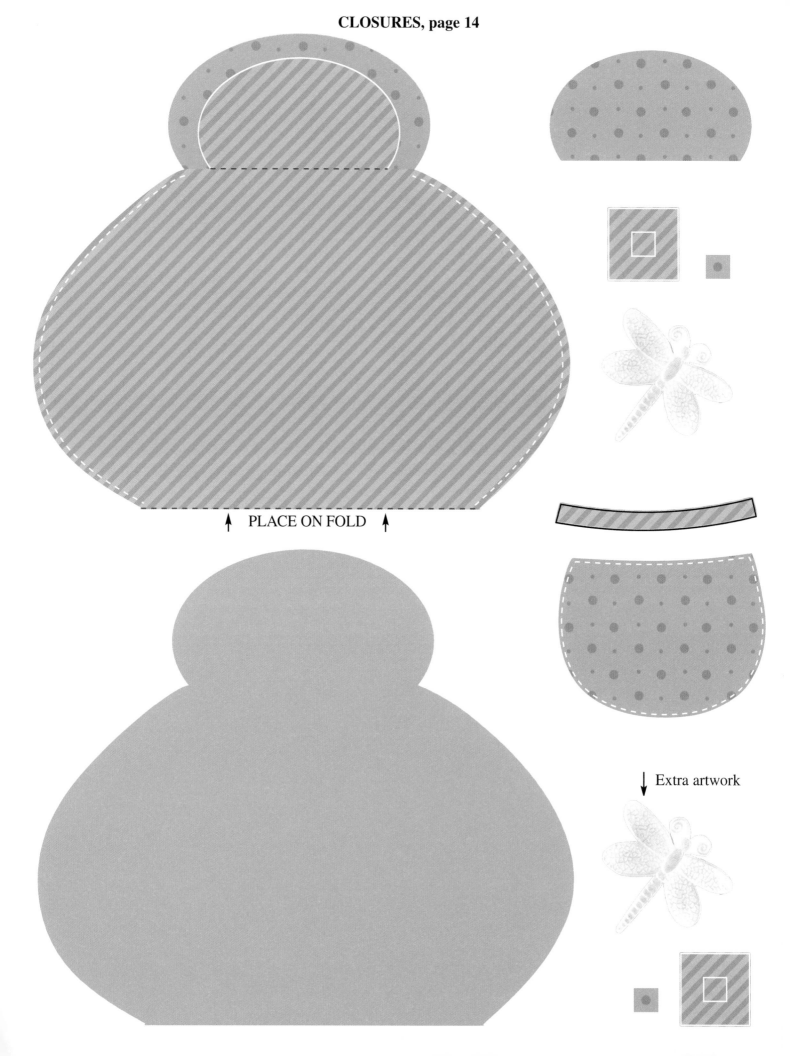

↑ PLACE ON FOLD ↑

↓ Extra artwork

COLLAGE,

Extra
artwork

Just for You!

Or write your own message here

Birthday Wishes

Or write your own message here

DANGLE, page 19

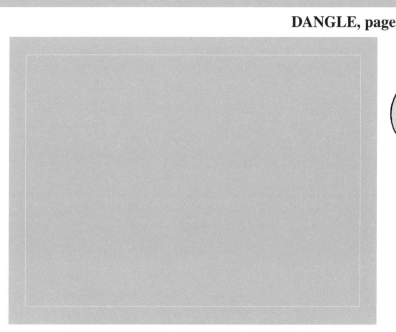

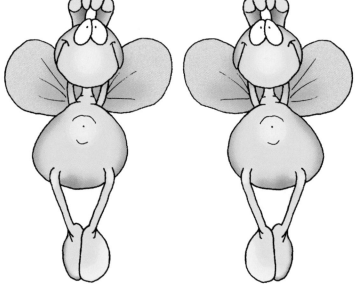

Hang in there!

And feel better soon!

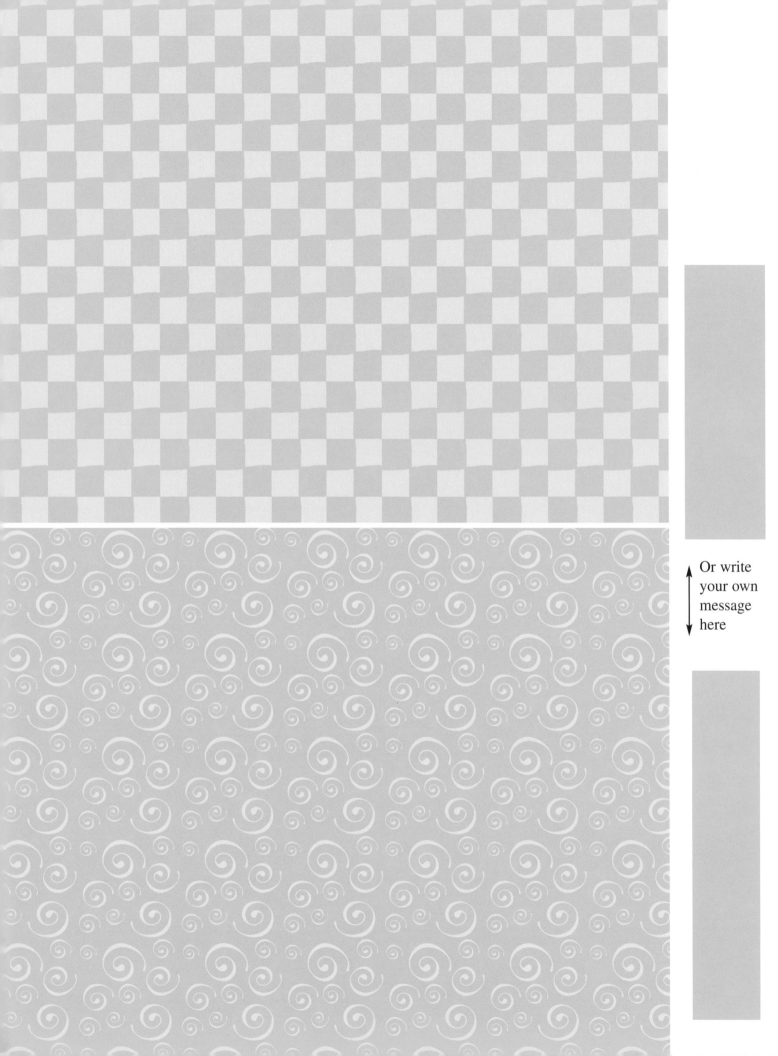

Or write
your own
message
here

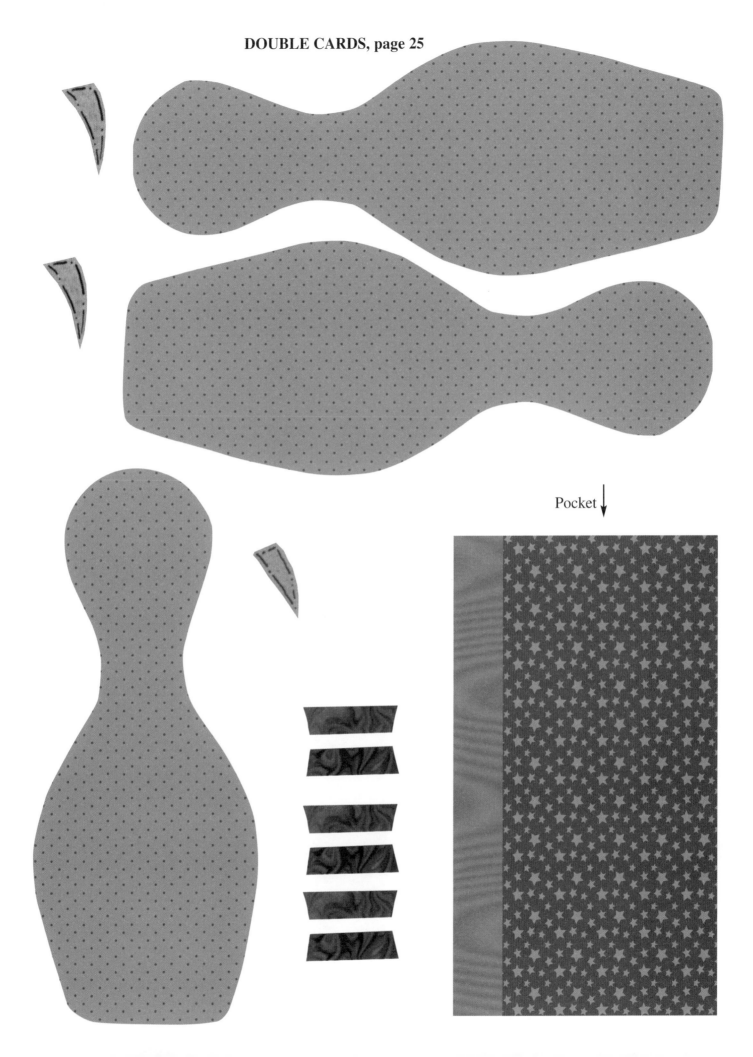

Pocket ↓

Would like to spend a moment with you if you have some "spare" time.

Or write your own message here

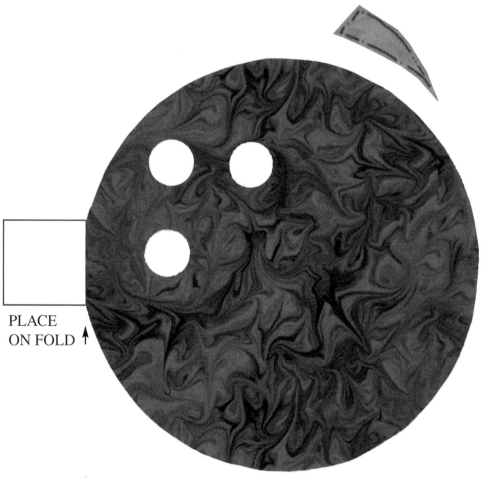

PLACE ON FOLD ↑

FOLD BACK, page 31

Thank You!

↓ Or write your own message here

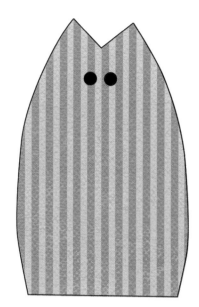

RIGHT HINGE, page 32

← PLACE ON FOLD

PLACE ON FOLD →

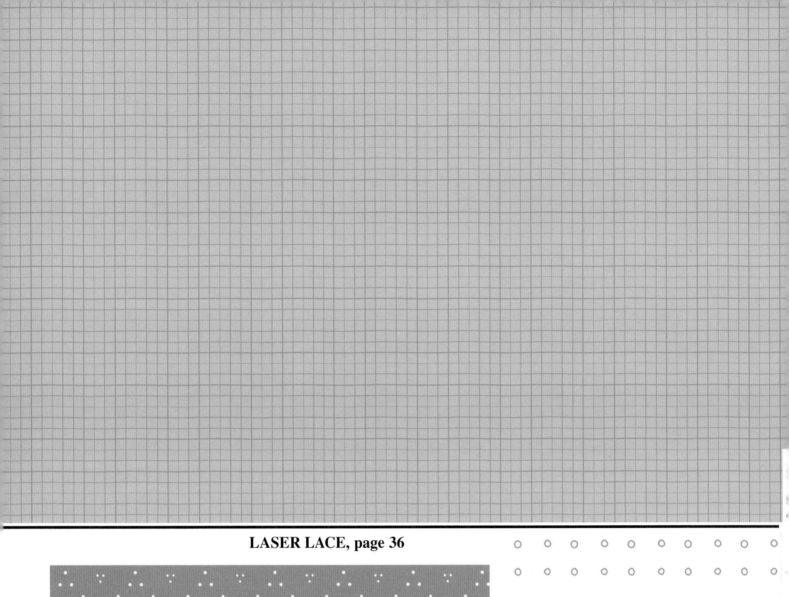

LASER LACE, page 36

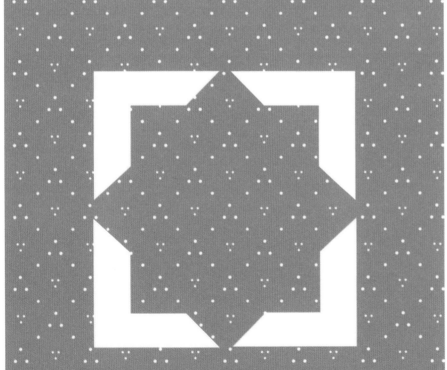

LATTICE CUTS, page 38

↓ Extra
Motif

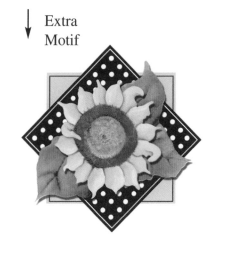

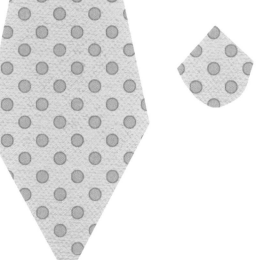

↓ PLACE ON FOLD ↓

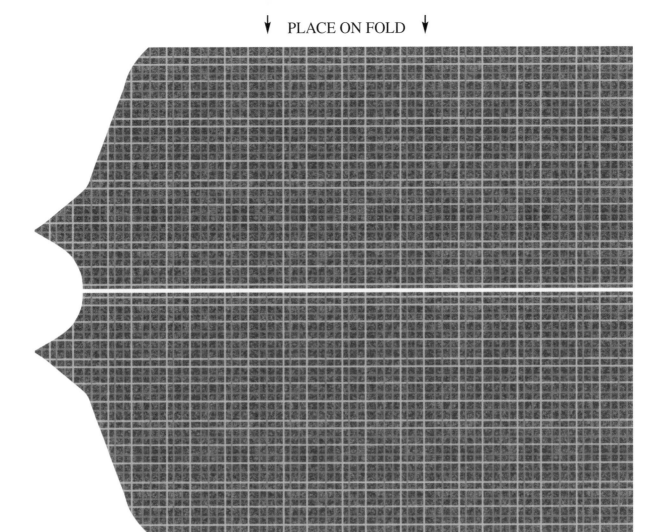

↑ PLACE ON FOLD ↑

PIN PRICKING, page 51

PIN PRICKING, page 51

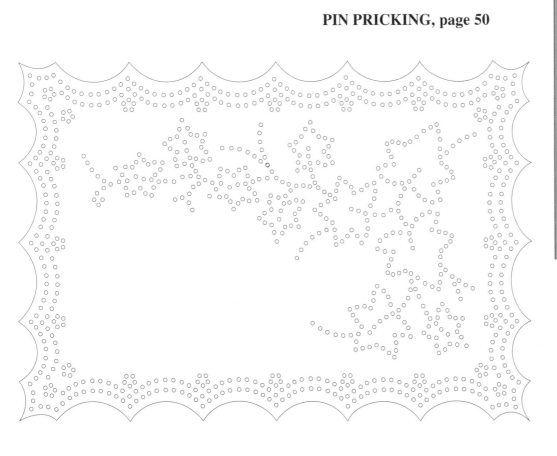

Best
Wishes

PIN PRICKING,
page 50

WHITE FOR MATTING

Happy
Birthday

Or write your own
message here ↓

Spring
has
Sprung!

Take time to
smell the
flowers!

Or write your own
messages here

FOLD

FOLD

PLACE ON FOLD

Extra butterflies

SUPPORT STRIPS

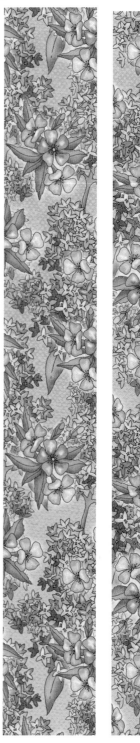
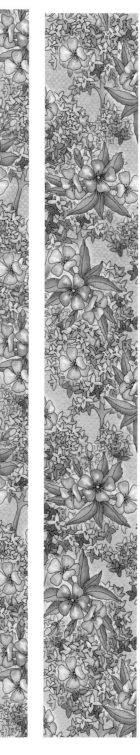

Sending you love

across the miles!

Or write your own
message here

PRESSED FLOWERS, page 54

Extra
Artwork

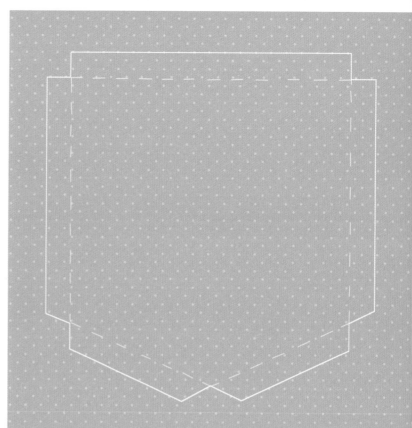

SHAPED, page 56

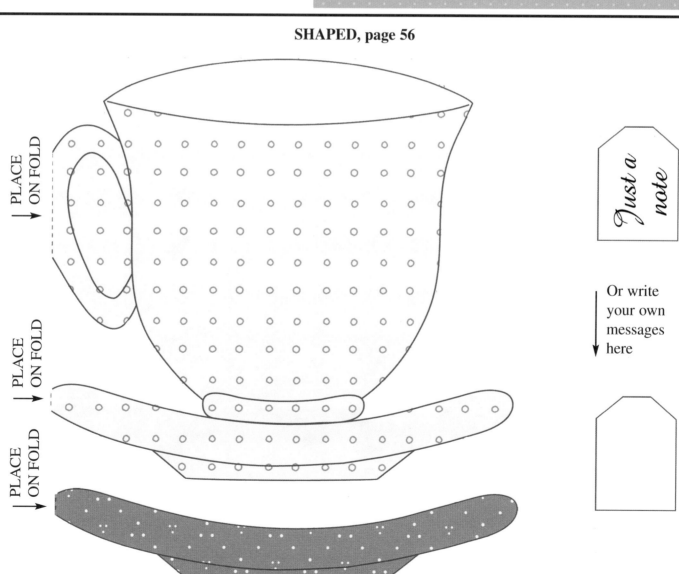

PLACE ON FOLD

PLACE ON FOLD

PLACE ON FOLD

PLACE ON FOLD

Just a note

Or write
your own
messages
here

SHAPED, page 56

HOWDY, PARTNER!

↓ Or write your own message here

↓ Extra star

HAPPY BIRTHDAY, COWBOY!

↓ Or write your own message here

PLACE ON
FOLD

3-D, page 66

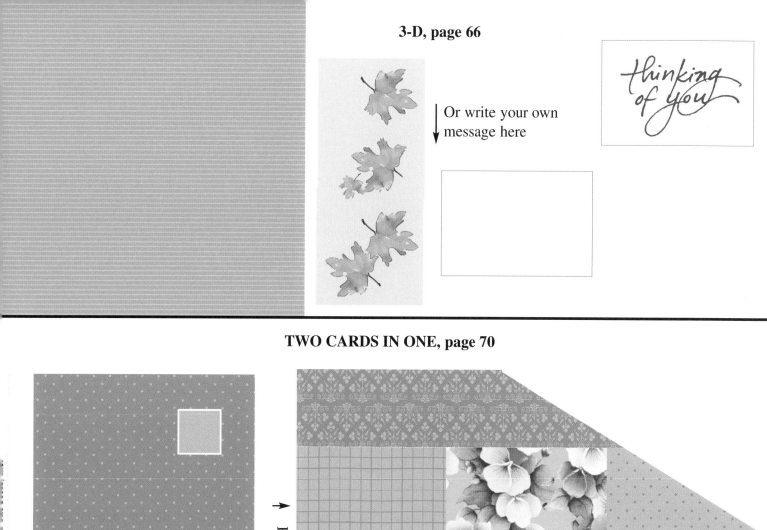

Or write your own message here

thinking of you

TWO CARDS IN ONE, page 70

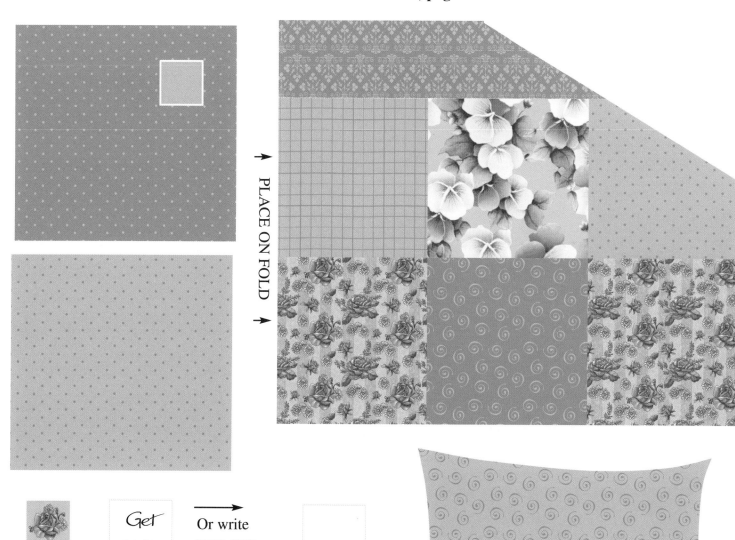

PLACE ON FOLD

Get Well Soon!

Or write your own message here

↓ White for matting pillow ↓